CONCILIUM
Religion in the Seventies

CONCILIUM, v. 98

New Series: Volume 8 Number 10: Ecumenism

CHRISTIANS AND JEWS

Edited by

Hans Küng and Walter Kasper

seminary library

Charles L. Souvay Memorial

A CROSSROAD BOOK

The Seabury Press • New York

The Seabury Press
815 Second Avenue
New York, N.Y. 10017

Library of Congress Catalog Card Number: 76-10050
ISBN: 0-8164-2095-5
Printed in the United States of America

CONTENTS

Editorial

JEWS and Christians rarely meet on a religious footing, and seldom engage in theological discussion with one another, despite the declaration of Vatican II on the Jews and the corresponding pronouncement of the World Council of Churches. There is still a considerable amount of hidden mistrust on both sides and, above all among Christians, a great deal of ignorance.

This section of our double issue of *Concilium* is intended to help forward the process of Jews and Christians learning to know one another better. Our intention is not to talk abstractly and generally about better or improved relations between Christians and Jews; and we don't intend to offer information about Judaism from a purely historical standpoint of the neutral science of religion, or history of religions. We wanted to get Jewish and Christian theologians round a table where they could talk to one another not only on a humanitarian basis but on the footing of their respective fundamental beliefs, quite objectively and fairly. In doing so they were to offer us information about the same central questions, in order to allow individual readers some basis for comparison and therefore a more profound reciprocal understanding of the present situation. To that extent and in that form the undertaking was entirely novel.

We have avoided anything like a summary of the results, which couldn't do justice to the number and complexity of problems involved. From the start this kind of theological dialogue cannot be an end in itself but only a beginning which has to be followed up on several levels.

Nowadays it seems impossible to compose a theological volume about Jews and Christians without adverting to the political fact of the State of Israel, which means an intermingling of theology and politics. Unfortunately the circumstances of the English publication of this issue of *Concilium* prevented the inclusion of a documentary report on the different Christian view of the modern State of Israel.

In general we should like to stress the fact that every author was left quite free to put forward his own opinion. And so every contribution represents only the viewpoint of its author. That is to say: *Concilium* has offered a forum for discussion but neither *Concilium* itself, nor its administrative committee, nor the particular editorial committee, takes up any specific position in this regard.

A final word: it seems almost superfluous to point out that there is no anti-Arab or anti-Islamic orientation to this issue of *Concilium*. On the contrary: it is intended to do its bit in forwarding understanding between Jews and Arabs, between Judaism and Islam. We hope shortly to produce a similar issue on Christians and Islam.

WALTER KASPER
HANS KÜNG

Translated by John Maxwell

Introduction:
From Anti-Semitism to
Theological Dialogue

I. THE AFFLICTIONS OF THE PAST

THE sufferings of the Jewish people begin with Jesus himself.[1] Jesus
was a man — that has always been more or less stressed by Christians,
who were less prepared to admit, however, that Jesus was a *Jewish* man
— a genuine Jew. As such he was far too often alien to Christians *and*
to Jews.

1. Jesus the Jew

Jesus was a Jew; a member of that small, poor, politically impotent
people on the fringe of the Roman Empire. He was active among Jews
and for Jews. His mother Mary, his father Joseph, his family and his
disciples were Jews. His name was Jewish (in Hebrew, 'Jeshua' — a late
form of 'Iehoshua': 'Yahweh is help'). His Bible, his divine service, and
his prayers were Jewish. In the existing situation it was impossible for
him to conceive of proclamation among the Gentiles. His message was
for the Jewish people: but for the entire Jewish people, without any
exception.

That is the basic situation: without Judaism there would be no
Christianity. The Bible of the early Christians was the Old Testament.
The New Testament writings became the Bible by attachment to the
Old Testament. The Gospel of Jesus Christ wholly (and quite consciously) presupposes the Torah and the Prophets. In both Testaments the
same God of grace and justice is speaking, even according to the Christian conception of things. This special relationship is the reason why I
do not consciously treat Judaism in the early chapters of my forthcoming book on Christianity — those deal with the non-Christian reli-

9

gions. Christianity does not enjoy this unique relationship with Buddhism, Hinduism and Confucianism, not even with Islam (influenced by Christianity), but only with Judaism. It is a relationship of the origins, and several common structures and values result from it. In that case we have to ask why, despite its universal monotheism, not Judaism but the new movement emanating from Jesus — Christianity — became a universal religion of mankind.

Enmity between very close relatives can be very bitter. One of the most tragic events in the history of the last two thousand years has been the enmity which existed between Jews and Christians almost from the start. It was reciprocal, as so often happens between an old and a new religious movement. Of course the young Christian community at first seemed no more than a special religious orientation within Judaism; and one which acknowledged and practised a special religious constitution, but otherwise upheld the connexion with Jewish national society. But the process of detachment from the Jewish national community was based inwardly on an acknowledgement of Jesus. It was very soon dissolved by the formation of a Gentile Christianity without the Law. Before long the Gentile Christians were in the overwhelming majority and their theology lost its real attachment to Judaism; After a few centuries the process concluded with the destruction of Jerusalem and the end of the temple cult. Hence in the course of a dramatic historical process the Church of Jews became and Church of Jews and Gentiles, and finally a Church of Gentiles.

Those Jews who did not wish to acknowledge Jesus were inimical to the young Church. They ejected the Christians from the national community and persecuted them, as the story of the pharisee Saul shows (who nevertheless as the apostle Paul always held to the specially chosen status of the people of Israel). It was probably by the second century that the cursing of the 'heretics and Nazarites' was included in the main daily rabbinical prayer ('Shmone "Esra" '). In short: the separation took place quite early on. The intellectual dispute was increasingly reduced to a continual struggle to find texts for or against the fulfilment in Jesus of the biblical prophecies.

2. A History of Blood and Tears

What happened after that was largely a history of blood and tears. The Christians who later won control of state power soon forgot the Jewish and Gentile persecutions they had suffered. Initially Christian enmity towards the Jews was not racially but religiously conditioned. More exactly, one should speak of 'anti-Judaism' instead of 'anti-Semitism'. Even the Arabs are Semites. In the Constantinian imperial Church the pre-Christian and Gentile anti-Judaism was adopted with 'Christian' emphases. And though subsequently there were instances of fruitful collaboration between Christians and Jews, the position of the Jews became much more sensitive, especially after the high Middle Ages. There were massacres of Jews in western Europe during the first two Crusades and pogroms in Palestine. Then there came the annihilation of three hundred Jewish communities in the German Empire in 1348-9 and the expulsion of Jews from England (1290), France (1394), Spain (1492) and Portugal (1497). And later there were the vile anti-Jewish speeches of the old Luther, persecutions of Jews after the Reformation, and pogroms in eastern Europe. During this period the Church certainly made more martyrs than it produced in its own ranks. All that seems incomprehensible for a present-day Christian.

Not the Reformation but humanism (Reuchlin, Scaliger), the Pietism (Zinzendorf) and especially the tolerance of the Enlightenment (the Declaration of the Rights of Man in the United States and in the French Revolution) prepared the way for a change and in part produced it. The full assimilation of the European Jews in the period of emancipation only succeeded in part, however, and most fully in America. It would be presumptuous to record yet again the century-long despicable history of the suffering and death of the Jewish people which culminated in the Nazi mass hysteria and murders which disposed of a third of all Jewry. The regret in the Vatican II declaration − which like a corresponding declaration of the World Council of Churches, is more of a beginning than an end − was extremely weak and vague in view of this vile history. It has been all but blocked by the Roman curia, which nevertheless got very heated about Hochhuth's highly problematic *The Representative* − as before, out of political opportunism and not fully suppressed anti-Jewish feelings the Vatican refuses diplomatic recognition to the State of Israel.

In view of this situation, which is by no means resolved, and a recalcitrant anti-Judaism in Rome and Moscow, but unfortunately also in New York and elsewhere, I must state quite clearly: Nazi anti-Judaism was the work of godless anti-Christian criminals; but, without the almost two-thousand-year-long pre-history of 'Christian' anti-Judaism which also prevented Christians in Germany from a convinced and energetic resistance on a broad front, it would not have been possible!

Even though some Christians were also persecuted and yet others − especially in the Netherlands, France and Denmark − effectively helped the Jews, if we are to grasp the question of guilt proficiently, the following must be taken into account: None of the anti-Jewish measures of the Nazis − distinctive clothing, exclusion from professions, the Nuremberg 'laws' forbidding mixed marriages, expulsions, the concentration camps, massacres, gruesome funeral pyres − was new. All that already existed in the so-called Christian Middle Ages (the fourth great Lateran Council was in 1215) and in the period of the 'Christian'

Reformation. What was new was the racial grounding of these measures — prepared by the French Count Arthur Gobineau and the Anglo-German Houston Stewart Chamberlain, and then carried through in Nazi Germany with cruelly exact organization, technical perfection and a terrible industrialization of death. After Auschwitz there is nothing to extenuate: Christianity cannot evade a full avowal of its guilt.

II. POSSIBILITIES FOR THE FUTURE

The latest most frightful catastrophe of the Jewish people and — as far as Christians were concerned — the unexpected revival of the State of Israel — the most important event in Jewish history since the destruction of Jerusalem and the Temple — shattered 'Christian' anti-Jewish theology: that pseudo-theology which falsely interpreted the Old Testament salvation history of the Jewish people as a New Testament history of divine condemnation, and overlooked the continuing choice of the Jewish people accepted by the New Testament, and referred to itself exclusively as the 'New Israel'. With the second Vatican Council a consciousness of this won a place in the Catholic Church as well. The idea of a collective guilt for the death of Jesus on the part of the Jewish people then or today was expressly rejected by the Council. The ancient widespread prejudices — Jews are 'money-grubbers', 'well-poisoners', 'Christ-murderers', 'God-killers', 'cursed and condemned to wander' — no one dares any longer to put them forward seriously. The psychological motives operative in anti-Judaism — group enmity, fear of foreign bodies, the scapegoat mentality, a counter ideal, disorientation of personality structure, mass hysteria — are now increasingly acknowledged. The implicit or explicit excuse that 'The Jews make mistakes as well', 'You have to understand everything in its historical context', 'It wasn't the Church itself', 'You have to choose the lesser evil' — is now obsolete. People recognize that the Jews form a community of fate that is in many respects mysterious and astonishingly persistent: a race and not a race, a linguistic community and yet not a linguistic community, a State and not a State, a people and not a people. A community of destiny whose religious secret for the believing Jew as for the believing Christian is a special vocation of this 'people of God' among the peoples of the earth. The fact that in this perspective the return of the Jews to their 'promised land' — with cruel sacrifices for the Arab Palestinians who have been there for centuries — also has a religious significance for many Jews is something that Christians should at least be aware of.

Whatever Christians (also those of Arab origins — who need our understanding) may think of the State of Israel, it is true that a Church which, as often in the past, preaches love and yet sows hatred, proclaims life and yet spreads death, cannot invoke Jesus of Nazareth as its founder.

Jesus was a Jew and all anti-Semitism is treachery towards Jesus himself. The Church too often stood between Jesus and Israel. It prevented Israel from acknowledging Jesus. It is time for Christians not only to preach 'conversion' to the Jews, but to 'convert' themselves: to an encounter which has hardly taken place, not only to a humanitarian but to a theological dialogue with the Jews, which could serve not 'mission' and capitulation but understanding, mutual help and cooperation, and − indirectly perhaps − even a growing understanding between Jews, Christians *and* Muslims, who of course (who could forget it?) by their own origins are as closely joined to the Jews as they are to the Christians. All this should take place through a common faith in God the Creator and the resurrection of the dead in acknowledgment of Abraham and Jesus, who both have an important place in the Koran. The prerequisites for a genuine dialogue between Christians and Jews, to whom Christianity, Islam and mankind as a whole owe the incomparable gift of a firm belief in one God, are at present (despite all the foregoing) as good as non-existent. An unconditional recognition of the religious autonomy of our admittedly rigorous and exacting Jewish partners is a presupposition of that.

(i) In Christianity, and especially in German and English or American exegesis, long before the Hitler period there was a new openness to the Old Testament's autonomy and accordance with the New Testament. The significance of the Rabbis for an understanding of the New Testament was also recognized. And in comparison with the Greek-Hellenistic world, people had begun to emphasize the strong aspects of Hebrew thought: the greater degree of historical dynamics, an holistic orientation, a faithful and positive attitude to world, body and life, hunger and thirst for justice, an orientation to the coming kingdom of God. All that contributed to the desuetude of the neo-Platonic, neo-Aristotelian and neo-Scholastic encrustation of Christianity. For the official Catholic Church the declaration on the Jews of the second Vatican Council was 'the discovery or rediscovery of Judaism and the Jews in their own right as in their significance for the Church' (J. Oesterreicher).

(ii) The spiritual situation of Judaism has changed considerably, especially since the founding of the State of Israel. There has been a decreasing influence of casuistic and legalistic piety, especially among the younger generation, and an increasing importance of the Old Testament in contradistinction to the earlier universal emphasis on the Talmud. Great Jewish minds of our century − women like Simone Weil and Edith Stein, men like Hermann Cohen, Martin Buber, Franz Rosenzweig, Leo Baeck, Max Brod, Hans Joachim Schoeps, and more indirectly Sigmund Freud, Albert Einstein, Franz Kafka and Ernst Bloch −

brought what was uniquely Jewish nearer to Christians. Hence the way was open for the present common scientific Jewish-Christian research into the Old Testament, the Rabbis and the beginnings of work on the New Testament (as a witness to the Jewish history of faith). It has also meant a more vital and more fundamental design of divine service on both sides which reveals a visible relationship reaching far beyond literary criticism and philology. There is no question: from the basis of his Judaism a Jew can discover aspects of the New Testament which as often as not escape the Christian. Inspite of numerous restrictions and difficulties, the consciousness of a common and not only humanitarian but theological Jewish-Christian basis is in the making. From the Jewish side as well there is a demand for 'a Jewish theology of Christianity and a Christian theology of Judaism' (J. Petuchowski). In any case, theological dialogue between Christians and Jews is shown to be much more difficult than that between separated Christians, which at least has a common basis in the Bible. The conflict between Christians and Jews on the other hand goes right through the Bible and splits it into two Testaments, of which one group prefers the first and the other the second. And is it ever possible to evade the particular point of controversy? Precisely he who appears to unite Jews and Christians separates them most fundamentally: Jesus the Jew from Nazareth. Can Jews and Christians ever reach an understanding about him? What is in question seems to be much more than 'two modes of belief' (M. Buber). That the Jews should surrender their unbelief in regard to Jesus seems just as unlikely as that the Christians should abandon their belief in him. For if they did so, the Jews would no longer be Jews, or the Christians Christians.

Dialogue about Jesus

The dispute seems unsolvable. Has Jewish-Christian dialogue about Jesus of Nazareth any meaning at all? But one might just as well ask: Wouldn't both sides gain something if in answer to a Christian readiness to reach understanding, on the Jewish side mistrust, scepticism and malice in regard to the figure of Jesus could be reduced, and instead it was possible to extend an historically objective judgment, genuine understanding and perhaps even a valuation of the person of Jesus? Recent progress cannot be ignored. A long list of authors and works on Jesus of Nazareth has been published in the last few years in the State of Israel. Of course there are many Jews who would accept at least the 'Jesus of culture' even though they rejected the 'Jesus of religion'. The cultural significance of Jesus is also acknowledged. Surely, too, it is very difficult for a modern Jew fully to take part in western culture without continually coming into contact with Jesus, even though only in the great works of Bach, Handel, Mozart, Beethoven, Bruckner, and western art in general.

But there is still the question of the religious significance of Jesus. Christians have acknowledged the religious significance of Judaism. Surely then Jews have also to face the problem of the religious meaning of Jesus, the last of the Jewish prophets. Even in the nineteenth century there was a respectable Jewish tradition which tried to take Jesus seriously as a genuine Jew, and even as a major witness to faith. At the turn of the century Max Nordau, the faithful colleague of the founder of the Zionist movement, Theodor Herzl, wrote: 'Jesus is the soul of our soul, just as he is the flesh of our flesh. Who then would wish to exclude him from the Jewish people?' In the first half of the present century came the first thorough studies of the figure of Jesus from the Jewish side, the various publications of Claude G. Montefiore, and the best-known Jewish book on Jesus by Jospeh Klausner, which on account of its use of the material from the Talmud and from mid-rash may be thought of as the beginning of modern Hebrew research into the life of Jesus. The important Jewish thinker Martin Buber stresses the word of Jesus as that of the 'great brother' who deserves 'a major place in the history of faith of Israel', which can be 'reduced to no conventional category'. The Jewish researcher into Jesus' life, David Flusser, points out that Jesus is a Jew addressing the Jews. A Jew can learn from him how he should pray, fast and love his neighbour, what is the meaning of the Sabbath, the kingdom of God and the Law. It was along this line that Schalom Ben-Chorin wrote his recent book *Our Brother Jesus. The Nazarene from a Jewish Viewpoint*: 'Jesus is certainly a central character of Jewish history and faith-history, but he is also a piece of our present history and our future, and no different from the prophets of the Hebrew Bible — whom we should not look on in the light of the past alone.'

That reveals the beginnings of a Jewish recognition of the Jewish Jesus, as Schalom Ben-Chorin puts it: 'I note his brotherly hand, which grasps mine, and follow him.' But he goes on: 'It is *not* the hand of the Messiah — that wounded hand, in whose lines the most profound suffering is engraved . . . The belief of Jesus unites us, but belief in Jesus separates us.' But surely it is that wounded hand that we need to interpret, to explain more profoundly.

It is not impossible that in the future more Jews will manage to recognize Jesus as a great Jew and witness to faith — as indeed a great prophet or teacher of Israel. The Gospels have a special fascination for some Jews. They show a Jew the possibilities lying within the Jewish faith itself. And surely Jesus is to be understood precisely as an individual symbol of Jewish history. The Jewish painter Marc Chagall always portrayed the suffering of his people in the image of the Crucified. Perhaps we ought to put it like this: Surely the history of this people

and its God, this people of tears and life, of lamentation and trust, culminates in the one figure of Jesus and his history as a spectacular sign
of the crucified and resurrected Israel?

And still one provocative question will remain: Who is Jesus? More
than a prophet? More than the Law? The Messiah? A Messiah crucified
in the name of the Law? Must discussion end quite unconditionally at
this point? It is probably here that a Jew could help a Christian: to conduct dialogue about Jesus not yet again 'from above', but 'from below'.
That would mean that we today also see Jesus from the perspective of
the Jewish contemporaries of Jesus. Even Jesus' disciples had at first to
start from the Jewish man Jesus of Nazareth and not from an already
proclaimed Messiah or Son of God. Only thus could they pose the question of the relation of Jesus to God. And that relation consisted for
them — at a later date as well — not in a mere identification with God,
as though Jesus were God the Father. Perhaps Jews could help Christians to understand more proficiently the central New Testament pro-
nouncements about Jesus and particularly his special titles, which enjoy
an eminently Hebraic background.

As always, if we start from the Jewish man Jesus of Nazareth, then
we find we can go quite a long way with an unprejudiced Jew. Finally
the ultimate decision for or against Jesus looks rather different than we
might expect from the viewpoint of the long contestation between
Christians and Jews. In this regard all we should do initially is to strive
for openness so that the unavoidable — Christian or Jewish — pre-under-
standing does not become prejudice. It is not neutrality that is wanted
but objectivity in the service of truth. In a time of basic reorientation
of the relationship between Christians and Jews we have to stay open to
all future possibilities.

HANS KÜNG

Translated by John Maxwell

Note

1   These observations form part of a complex of problems presented in my
introduction to Christianity (shortly to appear in English).

I The Significance of the Law

1 In Judaism

Louis Jacobs

IT is axiomatic that the Law — the Torah — is a key-concept in Judaism. No group of people professing the Jewish religion has ever abandoned this concept and remained within the faith, though differing interpretations of the scope and meaning of the Torah are found and stages in the development in the concept can be traced without too much difficulty. The doctrine that the 'Torah is from Heaven'[1] became very prominent as a basic Jewish belief but this doctrine itself did not drop down from Heaven ready made, as it were, but has had a long history.

I. THE TERM TORAH

In the Pentateuch, and in other parts of the Old Testament, the word *torah* refers generally to a particular law or teaching or to a group of laws or teachings.[2] It was only at a later date that the whole of the Pentateuch became *the* Torah[3] or the 'five books of the Torah'. In Rabbinic Judaism the term Torah embraces the Written Torah (primarily the Pentateuch but also the other biblical books) and the Oral Torah. This latter terms covers the instructions, laws and teachings given to Moses at Sinai, the hermeneutical principles by means of which Scripture is investigated for the purpose of drawing out its fullest implications, and the teachings of the sages in their attempt to further the process of Torah application. R. Levi b. Hama said in the name of R. Simeon b. Lakish: What is the meaning of the verse: 'And I will give thee the tables of stone, and the law and the commandment, which I have written that thou mayest teach them' (Exodus, 24.12)? 'Tables of

17

stone'; these are the ten commandments; 'the law'; this is the Pentateuch; 'the commandment'; this is the Mishnah; 'which I have written';
this is the Gemara. This teaches that all these were given to Moses at
Sinai'.[4] There is sufficient evidence that the idea of the Oral Torah was
conceived of in dynamic terms. New ideas, regulations and concepts
could be introduced by the sages and their disciples in the spirit of the
original Torah and these themselves then became part of the Torah.
'Whatever a keen disciple is destined to rehearse in the presence of his
master had already been given to Moses at Sinai.'[5] There are references
in the Talmud to disciples spying on the more intimate details of their
masters' lives and, when reprimaded, excusing their effrontery with the
plea: 'It is Torah and I am required to learn'.[6] How the ideal Jew
conducts himself in his daily life is part of the Torah.[7]

In Rabbinic interpretation, the scriptural references to *torah* were
understood as meaning the Torah in this far wider sense. On the verse:
'This is the law (*torah*), when a man shall die in the tent' (Num. 19.14)
a Rabbinic homily has it[8] that 'words of Torah are firmly established
only by the man who kills himself for it', i.e., by devoting himself to
the study of the Torah with complete self-denial. Another homily[9] on
the verse: 'With this (*be-zot*) shall Aaron come into the holy place'
(Lev. 16.3), concludes that the high priest is fortified to enter the Holy
of holies in the merit of the Torah which is called 'this' (*zot*), as in the
verse: 'And this (*ve-zot*) is the law (*torah*) which Moses set before the
children of Israel' (Deut. 4.44). The Biblical metaphor, in which the
relationship between God and Israel is seen as a marriage, is adopted
but varied. Israel is now the bridegroom with the Torah as the bride.
Thus there is a Rabbinic comment[10] on the verse: 'Moses commanded
us a law (*torah*), an inheritance of the congregation of Jacob' (Deut.
33.4). Here, too, the word *torah* is understood as referring to the Torah
as a whole, while the word for 'inheritance' — *morashah* — is read as
meorasah, 'a betrothed maiden', to yield the thought that the Torah is
Israel's betrothed. But since the Torah (= Scripture) can have many
meanings[11] the original reading of 'inheritance' is also retained to convey the thought that that the Torah is Israel's heritage. 'R. Juda said[12]
in the name of Rab: Whoever witholdeth a teaching (*halakhah*) from his
disciple it is as if he had robbed him of his ancestral heritage, as it is
written: 'Moses commanded us a *torah*, an inheritance of the congregation of Jacob', it is an inheritance destined for all Israel from the six
days of creation'.

Similarly, *hokmah* ('wisdom'), praised so highly in the book of
Proverbs, is identified not with wisdom in general but with the Torah.
'R. Nahman b. Isaac said:[13] Why are the words the Torah likened to a
tree, as it is said: 'It is a tree of life to them that grasp it' (Prov. 3.18).
It is to teach you that just as a small tree may set a bigger tree on fire

so, too, it is with scholars, the younger sharpen the minds of the older. This identification became so obvious that the verse: 'It is a tree of life' was incorporated into the synagogue liturgy,[14] and is still sung during the sabbath and festival services when the scroll of the Torah is returned to the Ark. Conversely, during the Middle Ages, among some teachers, philosophical studies were introduced not as rivals to the Torah but, insofar as the ideas were not heretical, as part of the Torah. The most determined defender of this view is Maimonides who, in a statement that was deeply offensive to the traditionalists, equated the 'Work of Creation' and the 'Work of the Chariot' referred to in the Talmud[15] (in the context, the mystical teachings contained in the first chapter of Genesis and the first chapter of Ezekiel, and belonging to the highest reaches of torah study), with, respectively, Aristotelean physics and metaphyscis.[16] The Kabbalists, on the other hand, read their own theosophical system into Scripture.[17]

II. THE IMPORTANCE OF THE TORAH

The Torah is the link between God and man. The ladder, seen by Jacob in his dream (Gen. 28.12), connecting heaven and earth is said to be Sinai[18] on which the Torah was given. The Torah was created before the creation of the world.[19] God consulted the Torah before he created the world as the architect consults his plans before he begins to build.[20] God rejoices that he has given to Torah to Israel.[21] The world only endures because of the Torah. If Israel had not accepted the Torah God would have turned the world back to emptiness and formlessness.[22] God himself studies the Torah[23] and he obeys its laws unlike the king of flesh and blood for whom, in the Greek proverb quoted by the Talmud,[24] 'the law is not recorded', i.e. does not apply. So precious is the Torah that it was desired by the angels in heaven who pleaded with God to give it to them and not tarnish it by giving it to mortals but God replies through Moses that the laws of the Torah are intended to help overcome human faults from which the angels do not suffer.[25]

The Torah is life-giving,[26] enriching and elevating man's life in this world and equipping him to enjoy eternal bliss in the Hereafter.[27] Typical is the rabbinic saying,[28] theoretical though it is, that a man guilty of accidental homicide, who is obliged to flee to one of the refuge cities and remain there in custody, can demand that his teacher comes to stay there with him, since Scripture says that he might live there (Deut. 4.42) and life without the Torah is no life. Eternal bliss is the reward of those who study the Torah and those who support the scholars. A favourite description of heavenly bliss is as the great College on High in which the Torah is studied.[29] A Rabbi who took too long over his prayers and so spent less time in study of the Torah was rebuked by his colleague for neglecting eternal life in order to engage in temporal existence.[30] Only those for whom the study of the Torah was the supreme religious duty could have given it such prominence over prayer, which the Rabbis themselves declare to be among those things that stand exceedingly high in the spiritual universe.[31] The ruling of the Mishnah[32] is revealing. If a man's father and his teacher who taught him the Torah are both held to ransom by bandits he must first save the teacher, because while the father brings him into this world the teacher brings him into the life of the World to Come.

The Torah is the antidote for the poison of sin.[33] In what is possibly a conscious reaction to the Christian doctrine of original sin,[34] a rabbinic saying[35] has it that the serpent copulated with Eve and infected her and her descendants with his filth but when Israel stood at Sinai to receive the Torah their filth departed from them. The evil inclination and its control by the Torah is expressed in the form of a parable.[36] A man struck his son wounding him but later placed a plaster on the wound. The father says to his son: 'My son! As long as this plaster is on your wound you can eat and drink at will and bathe in hot or cold water and no harm will come to you. But if you remove the plaster the wound will fester.' So God said to Israel: 'My children! I created the evil inclination but I also created the Torah as its antidote. If you occupy yourselves with the Torah you will not be delivered into his hand.'

Yet for all the panegyrics on the study and practice of the Torah and the role it plays in God's plan, the Torah is never an object of worship. It is the means of worshipping God, never a substitute for him. Even the hyperbolic statement[37] that God says: 'Would that they had forsaken me if only they had kept my Torah' means no more than there is healing for the soul in the bare study and practice of the Torah even when a religious motivation is absent. The statement, in fact, concludes: 'for the light of the Torah will bring them back to the good', that is, to God. Some mediaeval teachers[38] even objected to the harmless custom of bowing to the scroll of the Torah in the synagogue or of bowing to the Ark where the scrolls are kept. The nineteenth-century Hasidic master, R. Menahem Mendem of Kotak, could say that there is an injunction against making an idol of God's commands.[39] In the literature of Jewish piety there are numerous references to the love and fear of God and to the love of the Torah but nowhere is there to be found the term 'fear of the Torah' or other terms suggesting that the Torah is in any way an object of worship, nor is there any reference to prayers being offered to the Torah. The clear distinction is seen in the prayer of the third-century Babylonian teacher Rab,[40] later adopted as a pre-New Moon prayer,[41] which speaks of 'a life in which the love of the Torah and the fear of Heaven shall be with us'. In a well-known

Talmudic passage,[42] the Rabbis, interpreting the verse (Deut. 6.13) 'fear the Lord thy God', which contains the sign of the accusative — *et* — understood as including something else not mentioned in the verse, were puzzled as to what could be included, until R. Akiba said that it includes students of the Torah who have to be revered as God is. Evidently, no one thought that the Torah be included because if it were there would be the danger, obviously inapplicable to the inclusion of scholars, of according divine status to the Torah. The maxim generally attributed to the Zohar:[43] 'The Holy One, blessed be he, Israel and the Torah are one', can never have been intended to suggest the divinity of the Torah, as the inclusion of Israel in the maxim demonstrates.

Short of according divine status to the Torah, traditional Judaism has never faltered in affirming the Torah's centrality in God's creation. For the Rabbis, the good life is impossible without the Torah. Thus the Patriarchs are said to have kept the Torah before it was given.[44] For this reason, the Torah, while in its fullest range for Israel alone, is for Gentiles as well as for Jews. A Gentile who occupies himself with the Torah is equal to the High Priest,[45] the head of the priestly cast, the aristocrats. By the Torah for the Gentiles is meant the observance of the 'seven laws of the sons of Noah',[46] basic rules of conduct for all mankind, such as the prohibition of murder and theft and the need to have an adequate system of justice in the state. The Gentile who follows the Torah that is for him is counted among 'the righteous of the nations of the world' who have a share in the World to Come.[47]

As a corollary to the doctrine that the Torah is from God and the expression of his wisdom, is the doctrine that the Torah is immutable. Maimonides' ninth principle of the faith[48] understands this doctrine to mean not alone that Judaism will never be superseded by any other religion but that the laws of the Torah will never be changed and are binding for all time. There are, however, statements here and there in the rabbinic literature which suggest that some laws will be abrogated in the Messianic Age so that the mediaeval thinkers were at pains to qualify this apparent contradiction to the doctrine of the immutability of the Torah.[49] Among the early Kabbalists there appears the notion of cycles, each of 7000 years duration, in each of which there is a new Torah with different laws,[50] an idea strongly repudiated by the later Kabbalists and which resulted among the followers of the false Messiahs Shabbetai Zevi and Jacob Frank in a thoroughgoing antinomianism foreign to the Jewish tradition.[51]

III. DIFFERENCES IN MODERN JUDAISM

In contemporary interpretations of Judaism, the Torah continued to hold a central place. In every synagogue, anywhere in the world and of whatever denomination, the scrolls of the Torah repose in the Ark, the most sacred spot in the building. It has been said that Orthodox Judaism in the twentieth century stressed the idea of Torah, Conservative Judaism the idea of Jewish peoplehood, and Reform Judaism the idea of God. There is some truth in this generalization, but all three groups continue to affirm the centrality of Torah, though Conservative Judaism tends to be more flexible than Orthodoxy in its interpretation of the laws, while Reform Judaism attaches greater significance to the ethical and universalistic aspects of the Torah but with no rejection of many of the ritual laws. As for Jewish scholarship, numbers of modern Jewish scholars strive for objectivity in their study of the Torah, investigating the Jewish past and its literature, as they would any other branch of human culture, in a detached, 'scientific' manner rather than as a devotional exercise. Nonetheless, a large number of these scholars, too, are observant of the laws of the Torah and attempts have been made to see modern Jewish scholarship, for all its espousal of the critical approach with its freedom from bias, as a version of Torah study.

The fact that there is a special festival in the Jewish calendar called: *Simhat Torah*, 'Rejoicing of the Law', is sufficient evidence that the Jew in the present as well as in the past takes 'delight in the Law of the Lord'. And the evening prayer, recited by the devout Jew daily, expresses his love for the Torah: 'With everlasting love Thou hast loved the house of Israel, Thy people; a Torah and commandements, statutes and judgements has Thou taught us. Therefore, O Lord our God, when we lie down and when we rise up we will meditate on Thy statutes; yea, we will rejoice in the words of Thy Torah and in Thy commandments for ever; for they are our life and the length of our days, and we will meditate on them day and night. And mayest Thou never take away Thy love from us. Blessed art Thou, O Lord, who lovest Thy people Israel.'

Notes

1   Mishnah Sanh. 10:1; Sanh. 99a; Maimonides' eighth principle of the faith in his Commentary to the Mishnah, Sanh. 10:1. Cf. my *Principles of the Jewish Faith* (London, 1964), chapter 9, pp. 216-301.

2   E.g. Ex. 12.49; Lev. 6.2; 6.7; 7.7; Num. 19.14; Deut. 4.44; 17.11; 17.19; 31.9; 33.4; Is. 2.3; 51.4; Jer. 18.18; Hag. 2.11; Mal. 2.6-7; plural *torot* in Ex. 18.16; 18.20; Lev. 26.46; Ezek. 44.24.

3   This is probably the meaning of *Torah* in Psalm 119 and possibly in Mal. 3.22, both very late passages. Cf. Robert H. Pfeiffer, *Introduction to the Old Testament* (New York, 1941), p. 129; O. Eissfeldt, *The Old Testament An Introduction* (Oxford, 1966), pp. 155-6.

4   Ber. 5a.

5   JT, Peah. 2.4, 17a.

6   Ber. 62a, cf. Solomon Schechter, *Aspects of Rabbinic Theology* (New York, 1961), pp. 125-6.

7   Cf. G. Scholem, *Major Trends in Jewish Mysticism* (London, 1955), p. 344.

8   Ber. 63b.
9   Lev. R. 21.6.
10   Pes. 49b.
11   'There are seventy faces to the Torah' (Num. R. 13.16). 'It was taught in the School of R. Ishmael: "And like a hammer that breaketh the rock in pieces" (Jer. 23.29). Just as the rock is split into many splinters, so also one Biblical verse can convey many meanings' (Sanh. 34a).
12   Sanh. 91b.
13   Taan. 7a.
14   Singer's Prayer Book, new ed., p. 210.
15   Mishnah Hag. 2.1; Sukk. 28a.
16   Yad, Yesode Ha-Torah 4.10-13.
17   Zohar III, 152a.
18   Midrash Gen. R. 68.12, ed. Theodor-Albeck, p. 786, the numerical value of Sinai equalling that of *sullam*, 'ladder'; see Theodor's note 4.
19   Gen. R. 8.2, ed. Theodor-Albeck, p. 57.
20   Gen. R. 1.1, ed. Theodor-Albeck, p. 2.
21   Ber. 5a.
22   Sabb. 88a.
23   A.Z. 3b, cf. B.M. 86a.
24   JT R.H. 1:3, 57b.
25   Sabb. 88b-89a.
26   'Just as water is life to the world so are words of Torah life to the world' (Yalkut, Isaiah 480).
27   Ket. IIIb.
28   Makk. 10a.
29   Ber. 18b; B.M. 86a; Makk. 11b.
30   Sabb. 10a.
31   Ber. 6b.
32   B.M. 2:11.
33   B.B. 16a.
34   See E. E. Urbach, *The Sages Their Concepts and Beliefs* (Heb. title *Hazal*) (Jerusalem, 1969), pp. 371-92.
35   Sabb. 146a.
36   Kidd. 30b.
37   Midrash Lam. R. Introduction 2, cf. the different version in JT Hag. 1.7, 76a.
38   *Shilte Ha-Gibborim* to Alfasi, ed., Vilna Kidd, 14b.
39   *Ammud Ha-Emet*, Tel-Aviv, n.d., p. 44, though in this version the reference is said to be to carrying out the commandments without adequate concentration.
40   Ber. 16b.
41   Singer's Prayer Book, new edition, p. 205.
42   Pes. 22b.
43   Cf. Israel Bettan, *Studies in Jewish Preaching* (Cincinnati, 1939), p. 39, note 94.
44   See the sources and discussion in Louis Ginzberg, *Legends of the Jews* (Philadelphia, 1942), Vol. V, p. 259, note 275.
45   B.K. 38a.
46   See the comprehensive treatment in *Encyclopedia Talmudit*, Vol. III, *s.v. ben noah*, pp. 348ff.
47   Tosefta Sanh. 13.2 (ed. Zuckermandel).
48   Commentary to Mishnah Sanh, 10.1.
49   See, e.g., Albo's *Ikkarim*, Vol. III, chapters 13-23, ed. Husik (Philadephia, 1946), pp. 112ff for a full discussion of this problem.

50   See Israel Weinstock, *Be-Maagale Ha-Nigleh Ve-Ha-Nistar* (Jerusalem, 1969), pp. 151ff.
51   See G. Scholem, *The Messianic Idea in Judaism* (New York, 1971).

2 In Christianity

William Davies

TO a biblical student the study of Christian ethics in our time presents a confused spectacle. He cannot but be aware of a profound dichotomy within it. On the one hand, the Christian Gospel is understood in many ethical writings as a Gospel of liberation from Law, not only in its Jewish form, but, it would appear, in any form. Protestantism has witnessed a growing emphasis on an ethic without principles, an ethic governed by its context, often with little reference to the moral teaching of its foundation text, the Bible. Catholicism has often become critical of its own tradition of moral theology and casuistry and disenchanted with Law, canonical and other.

On the other hand, in biblical studies there has been in many quarters a growing appreciation of the significance of Law not only in the Old Testament but in the New. One of the most illuminating developments in Old Testament studies has been the rehabilitation of the Law. Through the work of Alt, von Rad, Noth, Clements and Buber and others, the influence of the Covenant with its Law even on the prophets, whom we were formerly taught to regard as the opponents of the priests and their Law, has become clear. The prophets are emerging as teachers of the Law. Zimmerli has given a fascinating account of all this in *The Law and the Prophets* (1956). And just as the prophets have been connected with the Law that preceded them, Finkelstein has linked them with the sages and with the Rabbinical Law that followed them. See Finkelstein, *New Light from the Prophets* (London, 1969).

All this has had an effect on New Testament Studies. But unfortunately Pauline polemic against the Law in Judaism and Jewish Christianity has so coloured the minds of Protestants and even Catholics that it has been difficult for them both to give its due place to the Law in the corpus of revelation. What was argued by Paul against the Judaic and Judaizing interpretation of the Law was applied to the whole structure of the faith. But at long last we are being delivered from this inability to do justice to the value of Law in the Biblical sources. We now see that the saving event of the Exodus, which gave birth to Israel, is indissolubly bound up with the obligation to obey certain norms of conduct, that is, certain demands made by Yahweh. And in the New Testament also the early Christians born of a new Exodus, in Christ, were conscious of being bound to certain legal norms which they sought to live by and put into practice.

It is from this perspective that I write here. Such a perspective confronts serious difficulties especially in the Pauline corpus. If I largely ignore these, it is not because I am not aware of them but because to deal with them would require more space than is available.

By 'the Law' I shall understand the moral demand made upon Christians and confine myself to the New Testament. This reveals varying emphases. Any neat presentation of early Christian teaching must immediately be suspect. But it is possible to indicate certain themes which convey the moral seriousness of the primitive Church.

I begin with a central fact: through the life, death and resurrection of Jesus of Nazareth, Christians believed that they were living 'in the end of the days', in the time of fulfilment of the expectations of Judaism (Is. 10.22; 34.4; 43.3; 45.17-22; 60.16; Gal. 4.4; Mt. 4.4, 6-7; 5.17-18; Mk. 12.28-37). This fulfiment did not ignore the moral content of these expectations. The early Church consciously accepted the moral concern of Israel as it was illumined and completed in the light of the life, death and resurrection of Jesus. Thus in much of the New Testament the experience of the Church was understood as parallel to that of the Jewish people. The emergence of the Church was, not indeed that of a new Israel, but the entrance of Israel on a new stage of its history. In the creation of the Church the Exodus was, as it were, repeated. As a corollary to the experience of a New Exodus, the Church understood itself as standing under the New Sinai of a New Moses. This complex of ideas largely governs Paul's references to the New Covenant (1 Cor. 11.23f), Matthew's presentation of the Sermon on the Mount, Mark's new teaching (1.27ff) and John's new commandment (13.34). What is clear is that 'Law', that is, moral demand, is bound up with the Christian Gospel, as it was bound up with the message of the Old Testament and Judaism. The structure of early Christianity is, in part at least, modelled upon or grows out of the structure of Judaism: that is, 'Law' is integral to the Gospel of the New Testament as it was to that of the Old. In both Testaments there is a 'way' (*hodos, halakah*) which the People of God is to follow.

But what is this 'way'? What 'law' is integral to the Gospel? This brings us to the motif that most governs the thought of early Christianity in morality. It reinterpreted the moral tradition of the Old Testament and Judaism in the light of Christ. It is the person of Christ that is normative for the understanding of morality in the New Testament. Just as early Christians reinterpreted the Temple, the Sabbath, Jerusalem and all significant symbols of Jewish self-identity in terms of Christ, so they reinterpreted the Law. They found 'in Christ' a new demand under which they stood, so that although the precise phrase does not occur – Christ became their 'Law'. I have urged elsewhere that Paul understood Jesus as taking the place of the Law. The demand of Christianity, that is, its Law, is concentrated in the Person of Christ.

This fact has three aspects which are exceedingly difficult to hold in proper balance. First, the moral life of Christians is moulded by the actual life of Jesus of Nazareth, that is, his ministry of forgiveness, judgment, healing, teaching, which culminated in the cross. Second, it has its point of departure not only in the ministry of Jesus but in his resurrection. The resurrection was the ground for the emergence of the primitive community but it was also the immediate inspiration of its morality. The resurrection was not only a triumph of life over death but of forgiveness over sin. It was an expression, perhaps *the* expression, of God's grace in Christ, because the risen Christ came back to those who had forsaken him and fled, who had slept during his agony. He forgave their failure. The resurrection as forgiveness emerges clearly in 1 Cor. 15.7ff; John 20.1ff. It was of a piece with the whole ministry of Jesus, and the morality of the community which it created was to be a morality governed by grace, that is, it was the morality of forgiven men who had known the risen Lord as a forgiving Lord, and who in gratitude, the most ethical of all the emotions, gave themselves to the good life in his name. Third, the mode of the presence of the risen Lord in the community was that of 'the Spirit'. The coming of the Spirit – not merely a wonder-working power but of moral dynamism – should never be separated from the resurrection as grace. Like the resurrection itself, the coming of the Spirit is 'an energy of forgiveness'. Thus it became the source of morality because gratitude for forgiveness is the ground of Christian being. Love, joy, peace, righteousness and every victory 'in the moral sphere' are the fruit of the Spirit. The enthusiasm of the Spirit found its true expression in *agape*.

When, therefore, we say that 'the Law' had been Christified, we mean that Christian morality had as its point of reference the life, death, resurrection and living Spirit of Jesus Christ: inextricably bound together, these were the source of the demand under which the early Church lived. And it is this that determines its manifold dimensions. These can be conveniently gathered together under two main heads.

I. VERTICIAL DIMENSIONS

We have seen that the ground on which the early Church stood was the life, death, resurrection and Spirit of Jesus Christ. To put the matter geometrically, it was their relation vertically to the Risen Lord, the participation of the early Christians in the experience of being forgiven by the Risen Lord and the Spirit, that lent them a common grace. They had been grasped by him and their response was primarily, through the promptings of the Spirit, to him. All Christian fellowship was rooted in a particular event — the life, death and resurrection of Jesus — and its morality is linked to the understanding of this event.

Now in much of the New Testament, though not in all, morality is understood in terms of the *appropriation* of this event, that is, the recapitulation of it in the life of the believer. The moral life is a life 'in Christ'; it is the living out in daily conduct what it means to have died and risen with Christ. This is true of Paul and possibly of Matthew. For Paul the act by which a Christian acknowledged his faith and really began to live 'in Christ' was baptism. This act symbolized a death to the old life under 'the Law' and a rising to newness of life 'in Christ' or 'in the Spirit'. By baptism the Christian through faith had died, had risen, had been justified: he was a new creation (Rom. 6.3; 1 Cor. 12.13; Gal. 3.27; 2 Cor. 8.9; 12.1; Phil. 2.5-8; Rom. 8.11). What was now necessary was for him to become what he was. His moral life is rooted in what he *is* — a new creation in Christ. Just as we call on each other 'to play the man', so Christians are called upon 'to play the Christian' — to *be* what they *are*. To use theological jargon, the imperative in Paul, is rooted in the indicative. There is a vertical dimension to Christian living — an attachment to the Living Person of Christ, his life, death and resurrection. So too in the Fourth Gospel the Christian is to re-enact the self-giving of God in sending Christ into the world. The 'love' which exists between the Father and the Son is to be reproduced in the relationships of the disciples to one another.

This vertical relationship has another aspect. Not only the imitation of God's act through dying and rising with Christ, but also the imitation of the 'Jesus of history' played a part in the moral development of the early Church. Early Christians looked to Jesus as their 'identifying figure'. Probably part of the reason for the preservation of stories about the life of Jesus, such as we have in the Gospels, was the desire to imitate Jesus in his acts. Christians were to take up the cross (8.34ff). While persecution (taking up the cross literally) was always a possibility, more often Christians were called to imitate their Lord in the witness of the common way, less spectacular perhaps, but no less arduous, than readiness to die — in love, forbearance, patience, mercy — in messianic grace. (Compare Mark 8.34 and Luke 9.23.) Christ is an object of imitation to Paul as Paul himself expects to be such an object to his own followers (1 Cor. 11.1). He holds up qualities of the historic Jesus which are to be imitated (Rom. 15.3; 2 Cor. 10.1; 2 Cor. 8.8-9). The description of *agape* in 1 Cor. 13 probably rests on the life of Jesus. For Paul every Christian is pledged to an attempted moral conformity to Christ. (Christ the Lord for him was not to be separated from the Jesus of history.) So too in the Fourth Gospel (John 13) and 1 Pet. 2.2; 4,1ff., the life of Jesus is a paradigm of the Christian life.

There is a third aspect to the vertical dimension of Christian living. The Christian is also taken up into the purpose of God in Christ. To be a believer is to be directed to and by Jesus of Nazareth as the Messiah. That is, there is always an *eschatological reference* to Christian living: the Christian shares in the purpose of God in the salvation revealed in Jesus to be completed in the future. In the light of the redemptive purpose revealed in Christ, they made their decisions, they discerned the things that further and that hinder that purpose and they became fellow workers with God. The life of Christians was sustained by the hope of the end, even as it was informed by the earthly Jesus. It was governed by a memory and an anticipation, 'a lively hope'.

II. HORIZONTAL DIMENSIONS

Early Christians were not exclusively oriented to the vertical realities indicated above. Early Christian morality contained an horizontal — a human, societal dimension. It is a morality born of the grace of the resurrection. The New Testament knows nothing of solitary religion and nothing of an individual morality — if, indeed, there be such. It points to a community with a life to live. This community was not to luxuriate in grace, absorbed in irrelevant, vertical privileges. As a community of grace, it took practical steps to give expression to grace in its life. How? We may summarize the answer under two main heads:

III. CHRISTIAN COMMUNITY

First, there was a constant concern among early Christians for the quality of their common life. This led to the experiment of the 'communism' of the early chapters of Acts; it was the natural, spontaneous expression of life in the Spirit. This appears from the naivete of the experiment. It failed, not to be repeated in this form, but it witnessed to the societary or communal morality of the primitive community in its realism and its unpracticability. That experiment took place in the light of an absolute demand for *agape* informed by the intensity of the Church's experience of forgiveness and, therefore, of grace.

This emphasis on the communal nature of the Christian way persists throughout the New Testament. It is rooted in a communal emphasis found in Jesus' choice of the Twelve, the nucleus of the new community. It is from this that here developed probably Paul's 'Christ-mysticism' which issued not in 'a flight of the alone to the Alone', but in building up the Church. Along with rationality (1 Cor. 12.8; 14.13ff; Rom. 12.2) Paul sets forth as the criterion of Christian action the building up of the Church. In the Johannine literature the love of the brethren is a mark of the Church.

IV. SPECIFIC MORAL TEACHING

At first, in the awareness of its resources in grace, the church attempted to live in the light of certain moral absolutes. These absolutes constitute the peculiarity, though not the totality, of the teaching of Jesus. Under inevitable pressures it became necessary for the Church to apply those absolutes to life. There began an attempt to transform the absolutes into practical rules of conduct, a Christian casuistry (see e.g., Mt. 5.32ff). This did not only occur in Jewish-Christian circles. The Pauline letters also appeal to the words of Jesus as authoritative. These words were at least one source of Paul's moral teaching. Two factors emerge clearly.

A. Paul interweaves words of Jesus almost unconsciously into his exhortations which means that these words were bone of his bone (compare Rom. 12;14; 12.17; 13.7; 14.13; 14.14; 1 Thess. 5.2; 5.13; 5.15 with Mt. 5.43; 5.39; 22.15-22; 18.7; 15.11; 24.43-44; Mk. 9.50; Mt. 5.39-41 respectively).

B. There was a collection of sayings of the Lord to which Paul appealed (1 Cor. 7.10ff; 9.14; 11.23ff; 14.37; 1 Thess. 4.15-16). Not only in legislative matters did Paul find guidance in the words of Jesus, but in personal matters (Rom. 7). In 1 Cor. 7.25 a word of Jesus is a commandment (*entole*): in two places we hear of the Law (*nomos*) of Christ (Gal. 6.2; 1 Cor. 9.20-22. See also Rom 8.2). This is no declension to a primitive legalism but the recognition of the role of the words of Jesus (John 14.25-26). Sometimes the words of Jesus are summed up in one word − *agape* (Mt. 7.12; Rom. 13.8-10; 1 Cor. 8.1; 13; Col. 3.14; John 13.34-35; 1 John 3.1; 2.7-10; 4.7-16). The expression of love is multiple, but its essential nature is revealed in Christ's dying for men. It is this kind of act that is demanded of those who love.

The necessity which led to the application of the absolutes of Jesus to life led the Church to take over for its own use codal material from Hellenism and Judaism. Most of Paul's letters and others reveal a two-fold structure: a first part dealing with 'doctrine' and a second dealing with 'morality'. Romans is typical. Chapters 1-11 are doctrinal: 12.1ff deals with moral questions. The catechetical origin of much in the 'moral sections' of the epistles is clear: they are largely drawn from instruction to converts at baptism. The presence of the imperative participle (e.g., in Rom. 12.9-10), a form found, but not common, in Hellenistic Greek but familiar in Hebrew legal documents, suggests that Paul and other Christian writers, drew upon codal material, such as is found in the Dead Sea Scrolls (DSD 1.18ff), the Mishhah Demai and Derek Eretz Rabba and Zuta. There are parallels also in Hellenistic sources. The early Church took over much pagan moral convention from the Jewish Diaspora: it borrowed from non-Christian sources: it not only domesticated the absolutes of Jesus but took over domestic virtues from the world.

This brings us to the last aspect of the New Testament moral teaching. That the Church was able to draw upon moral teaching from Judaism and Hellenism means that there was a continuity between the moral awareness of Christians and of the non-Christian world. Wherein did this continuity lie? It lay probably in the doctrine of creation which the early Church held. In the New Testament creation and redemption are congenial, as indeed in Judaism. The messianic age had cosmic dimensions for Judaism. So too in the New Testament the Creator and the Redeemer are one. Jesus can discover redemptive spiritual truths in the natural order (Mt. 5.43-48; and the parables), Paul finds in Christ the Wisdom, the creative agent of God, and John and Hebrews can find in him the Word by which all things were made. For the New Testament writers the good life is the truly natural life. Morality is rooted in creation.

V. THE LAW OF CHRIST

In summing up, what, then is the demand or Law of Christ as the New Testament understands it? There are specific commands of Christ, a body (though not to be utterly strictly defined) of moral teaching, a moral Messianic Law which was regarded as bringing 'the Law' of Judaism to its final form. Elements of this teaching, although simple in their forms, were stark in their demands, inescapable in their penetration and, apparently, impossible of fulfilment. Other elements were more 'ordinary', prescriptive, catechetical and parainetical. It is impossible to delete the prescriptive commandments from the New Testament. Christians brought with them to any situation which they faced a body of moral prescriptions and insights. They were not only, as were others, open to the demands of the context in which they moved, but they confronted that context with demands under which they stood. The New Testament also reveals moral casuistry. In addition, it borrowed concepts in the interpretation of 'The Way', from the surrounding culture, pagan and Jewish.

But the prescriptive casuistry which was present was never very highly developed: it remained uncomplicated. It was never in danger of becoming the kind of casuisitry against which Pascal wrote in the *Lettres Provinciales*, that in which practical ethics had become so befogged by fine distinctions and alternately meaningless definitions that it had ceased to be ethics of any kind, either practical or theoretical. This was because in the New Testament the moral teaching of Christ was not given autonomous centrality, but always understood in the total context of the *agape* of the life, death and resurrection of Christ and of the Spirit. The very commandments of Christ were subordinated to him. The self-giving exemplified in the cross was normative for all behaviour even in obedience to his commandments. All the demands of God in Christ are placed under his rule, that is, are informed by *agape* which may be defined, in part at least, as openness to suffering and moral sensitivity. But — and this is important — *agape* itself needed to preserve, and even to protect itself in terms of, prescriptions, which can both express *agape* and be a support for *agape*.

Now to isolate and emphasize the prescriptive elements in the New Testament is to risk a narrow, rigid, parochial legalism: to isolate the motif of the indicative-imperative is often so to individualize and 'spiritualize' our interests as to endanger our moral concern. Only the sober realism of the prescriptions — themselves, however, kept captive to the obedience of Chriat — can keep the indicative-imperative relationship healthy. We need what Leo Baeck called 'the cleanliness of the commandment'. So too the 'imitation of Christ' can become banal, archaic and 'hippyish' if taken in isolation. Even the cross itself can become, in isolation, a distortion of 'the Way', a warming of one's hands at the fires of martyrdom for one's own sake. The elements of the moral teaching of the New Testament are all to be interrelated, in this interrelationship is their strength and health, their mutual correction and their safeguard against misleading distortion and enthusiasm.

Finally, it is not superfluous to point out the relevance of all the above to the current ethical debate. Those who favour a prescriptive ethic are impatient with the contextualists who emphasize the free response of *agape* in the *koinonia*. In between these extremes are those who favour 'middle axioms'. In the light of the New Testament the debate is unreal or misplaced. Each school can find support for its position in the New Testament. What is more important, they can all find themselves corrected there in the rich totality of the New Testament Church, where Law 'prescriptive morality', *agape* and *koinonia* morality and middle axions all co-exist in mutual inter-action. The relevance of the genius of the moral tradition of the New Testament is that it holds all these approaches in living and healthy tension. In short, I plead for the recognition of the place of Law in Christianity but that within the context of the *total* canon.

Bibliography

Davies, W. D., *The Setting of the Sermon of the Mount* (Cambridge, 1965).

Davies, W. D., *Paul and Rabbinic Judaism* (London, 1970).

Carrington, Philip, *The Primitive Christian Catechism* (Cambridge, 1940).

Furnish, V. P., *Theology and Ethics in Paul* (Nashville, 1968).

Gustafson, J. M., 'Christian Ethics' in *Religion*, ed. Paul Ramsey (Englewood Cliffs, N.J., 1965).

Also the works of R. Schnackenburg, especially the excellent work, *The Moral Theology of the New Testament* (London, 1965), and for recent discussion those of J. A. T. Robinson. For further bibliography see my article on *The Ethics of the New Testament: Interpreter's Dictionary of the Bible*, E-J; and articles in *Neotestamentica et Semitica: Festschrift for Matthew Black* (Edinburgh, 1969), pp. 30-49, and *The Old Testament in the New, Festschrift for W. F. Stinespring* (Duke University, 1971). J. Moltmann, *Theology of Hope on the Ground and the Implications of a Christian Eschatology* (London, 1967); O. Cullmann, *Salvation in History* (New York, 1967); D. M. Stanley, ' "Become Imitators of Me": The Pauline Conception of Apostolic Tradition', *Biblica*, 40 (1952), pp. 859ff.

II Liturgy

1 The Structure and Contents of Jewish Liturgy

Joseph Heinemann

JEWISH liturgy developed gradually during the period of the Second Temple. Regular services — which came to be looked upon as a new form of 'worship' (*'abodah*), independent of, and equivalent to, the sacrificial cult performed in the Temple — were held, though at first in a variety of different forms. Some 'orders of prayers', especially the *'amidah* prayers for Sabbaths and Festivals and presumably also the weekday *'amidah*, the so-called 'Eighteen benedictions', were already customary in a more or less fixed structure in wide circles, prior to the destruction of the Temple. However, only in the days of Rabban Gamliel II, in the generation following the destruction, were these and other prayers given normative status and became (almost) fixed, as far as their order and structure was concerned; however, their wording remained fluid and changeable till at least the fifth or sixth century. By the time of the redaction of the *Mishnah* (end of the second century C.E.), practically all obligatory prayers had been definitely fixed; all further development since has been concerned merely with their further embellishment through poetic insertions (*piyyut*) and the addition of further rubrics, not strictly obligatory (though the latter, too, have become eventually fully established by custom — which in this area, however, differs widely from rite to rite).

I. SCRIPTURAL READINGS

The Synagogue service is composed of two constituent parts: prayers and readings from the Bible. Among the latter, the most important are readings from the Pentateuch, read in its entirety and consecutively in weekly portions allocated to each Sabbath, the first sections of which are also read in the morning services of Mondays and Thursdays (for the benefit of the country folk who would on those days attend the markets). In addition appropriate selected portions were also read on all Festivals, New Moon-days and fast-days. Such readings were regulated already by the Mishnah, as regards the number of people called to read on each occasion, the minimum number of verses to be read and, especially, the exact rules regarding the Torah-scroll to be used (which must be written in certain ways, on parchment etc.). However, the exact division of the Pentateuch into weekly portions was not uniform, at least till the third century C.E., and differed in each locality (cf. J. Heinemann, 'The Triennial Lectionary Cycle', *JJS* XIX, 1968, pp. 41-8). Eventually the so-called triennial cycle was adopted in Palestine, which was completed apparently in over three years; hence the same portions were read in different cycles in different seasons of the year. Even as late as the seventh century several forms of this lectionary were in vogue. In Babylonia the annual cycle, in which the entire Pentateuch is read in a single year — concluding and starting on the last day of the Tabernacles — was adopted; from there it spread to all present-day rites.

In addition, selected sections from the Prophets are read on Sabbaths and Festivals; the selection differed greatly in Talmudic times, and does so still today in some cases in different rites. On Purim, the reading from the Scroll of Esther is prescribed. Later custom introduced also the reading of Lamentations on the Ninth of Ab, and of the Song of Songs, the Book of Ruth and Ecclesiastes on Passover, Pentecost and Tabernacles respectively. From very early times, all readings were accompanied by *Targum*, i.e., rendering into the Aramaic vernacular, given orally verse by verse.

On most Festivals, the *Hallel*, consisting of Pss. cxiii-cxviii, is recited (in this case, there is no rule that it has to be read from a written text). Undoubtedly, psalms were used in the liturgy also on other occasions; but their recital was not obligatory. Nowadays, the morning prayer proper is preceded by a selection of 'songs', mostly consisting of psalms; but in Talmudic times this section was not part of the statutory liturgy.

II. THE PRAYER-SERVICES

However — notwithstanding their importance, formal scripture-readings are not an integral part of every service (and even where they occur they constitute, in fact, a separate unit). Hence ordinary services are made up of prayers — of praise, of petition and of thanksgiving. On weekdays three such services are held: in the morning, afternoon and evening on Sabbaths and other days on which additional sacrifices were offered in the Temple (cf. Num. XXVIII-IX), an additional service (*musaf*) is added after the morning-prayer. On the Day of Atonement (and, at the time of the Mishnah on all public fast-days), a fifth, 'concluding' service (*ne'ilah*) is recited just before nightfall. Individual worshippers, who do not, or cannot, attend a synagogue, recite the same prayers (omitting only some special sections, which may be recited only when a quorum of ten is present, cf. below; such a quorum is also required for the public reading from Scructure, discussed above).

All prayers which are part and parcel of the statutory services have for their distinguishing mark, which sets them apart from individual or optional prayers, the use of the *berakhah* (benediction), which opens with the stereotype formula 'Blessed art Thou, O Lord our God, King of the Universe', followed by some expression of specific praise, e.g., 'who redeems Israel', 'who has chosen us from among all nations and given us His Torah', etc. No constituent part of the obligatory prayer lacks this formula, either at its opening or its conclusion, or both (with the sole exception of the *qaddish*, see below); even the scripture-readings which are part of the prescribed service (see above) are placed in a framework of such benedictions which precede and follow them. Conversely, the use of the *berakhah*-formula is not authorized in private, non-statutory prayers where it is considered 'a *berakhah* recited in vain'.

However, while the use of the *berakhah*-formula in one way or another is mandatory in each unit and the number of such units and their main contents were regulated precisely, there remained nevertheless in Jewish prayer an element of spontaneity and individual freedom, viz. the exact wording of each constituent prayer. Not only was no definite wording prescribed in early Talmudic times; but the Sages objected to a prayer-leader (or individual worshipper) who would recite, time and again, the same words mechanically without 'saying anything new' in his prayer, 'as if he was reading from a letter'. 'The Synagogue strove to retain and to reconcile in its prayers both the requirement of agreement and informality . . . there continues for generations the deliberate tendency to keep the prayer fresh and fluid, modified with something new each day . . .' (S. Spiegel, in *The Jews*, ed. L. Finkelstein, Philadelphia, 1949, p. 539). Only during the last thousand years was the liturgy finally committed to writing and thus given a definite, prescribed wording (which, however, differs in details to this day among the various communities and their respective rites).

III. THE 'AMIDAH

Each of the daily prayer-services has at its core the *'amidah*, 'the prayer' par excellence, with the sole exception of the evening-service, where the *'amidah* is not obligatory (but is, nevertheless, recited invariably on the strength of a custom over a thousand years old). The exceptional position of the evening-service is probably due to the ancient concept which considers the *'amidah*-prayers to correspond to the sacrifices, viz. to the two daily sacrifices in the morning and evening respectively, and the *musaf-'amidah* on Sabbaths, and so on, to the additional sacrifices; but there is no sacrifice at night. Many of the services, such as the afternoon and the *musaf* service, consist in fact of the *'amidah* exclusively (and even though, nowadays, the latter is preceded by Psalms and the like and followed by the *qaddish* — see below — none of these belonged originally to the statutory prayers). In fact, the *'amidah* is recited twice in each community-service: first silently by each worshipper, and again aloud by the prayer-leader (with some additions, especially the *qedushshah*; see below); the purpose of the repitition was originally to enable those worshippers unable to recite the prayer by themselves, to 'fulfill their duty' by listening to its recital and responding with *Amen* after each *berakhah*. Hence, in the evening service, where the *'amidah* is not obligatory, it is not repeated aloud.

In structure, the *'amidah*-prayers for different occasions differ widely. While all have in common the first three benedictions (praising God for his greatness, his might — which finds expression especially in his ability to revive the dead — and his holiness) and the last three (which include the thanksgiving benediction and, finally, the prayer for peace, these six benedictions provide the framework for only one intermediate benediction on Sabbath and Festivals, but for twelve (nowadays: thirteen) petitions on weekdays. Notwithstanding their structural diversities, all *'amidah*-prayers have the same liturgical status. The one intermediate benediction for Sabbath etc. is concerned with the 'sanctification of the day', i.e. it expresses thanks to God for having granted us the Sabbath etc. Incidentally, the prayer in the *Constitutiones Apostolorum* (VIII, chps. 33-38) clearly reflects in structure, contents and even some phrases the first six of the seven benedictions of the *'amidah* for Sabbath, in spite of christological themes which have been interwoven into it (cf. K. Kohler, *Huca* I, pp. 411ff). Some Rabbinic sources suggest that on Sabbaths and Festivals all petitions have been omitted, because when praying for his needs man is liable to recall all his troubles and thereby to impair the joy of the Sabbath. However, other Sabbath and Festival prayers do contain at least petitions for the messianic redemption and grace after meals even on Sabbath has the petition for sustenance. Hence it appears more likely that the Sabbath-*'amidah* is actually of an earlier date than the 'Eighteen benedictions' and never did contain any petitions at all.

IV. THE EIGHTEEN BENEDICTIONS

The twelve (thirteen) petitions on the weekday *'amidah* are divided into two groups. The first is concerned with general, human every-day needs, such as the requests for forgiveness of sins, for the healing of the sick, the blessing of the crops (including, in the rainy season, a request for rain). The other contains petitions of national concern, viz. the in-gathering of the exiles, the re-building of Jerusalem, the restoration of the Davidic Kingdom — all of them giving expressions to various aspects of the messianic salvation. Among these latter is found the 'Benediction against the Heretics', which underwent many changes. Before the destruction of the Temple it was directed, apparently, against the 'wicked Kingdom', i.e., Rome, and against its Jewish collaborators. In the days of Rabban Gamliel II, it was aimed primarily against Jewish heretics, who included, undoubtedly, also Judeo-Christians; its purpose was to force such sects out of the synagogues, since they could not very well participate in prayers, which contained a curse directed against themselves; This benediction is not the additional one, through which the Eighteen Benedictions became nineteen: the texts in the Cairo *Genizah* have made it absolutely clear that the old Palestinian weekday *'amidah* never did have nineteen benedictions, even though it included, of course, the Benediction against the Heretics. The 'missing' benediction is the petition for the restoration of the Davidic Kingdom, which is included in the one for the building of Jerusalem. The additional, separate *berakhah* requesting the return of a Davidic King appears to have become customary in Babylonia and have spread from there to all present-day rites. Nevertheless, it would appear to be of Palestinian origin (even though it was not, in the end, accepted there); for it is suggested in Sirah LI and also appears to be reflected in Luke I, 68.

V. THE SHEMA' AND ITS BENEDICTIONS

The other major constituent part of the morning and the evening services is the Reading of the *Shema'* (= 'Hear, O Israel'; i.e., Deut. VI. 4-10, followed by Deut. XI. 13022 and Num. XV. 37-41). This reading is considered the 'proclamation of faith' in the One God and 'the Acceptance of the Yoke of the Kingdom of Heaven'. Because of Deut. VI. 7 ('when thou liest down and when thou risest up') its recital is mandatory both in the morning and in the evening. However, since a Biblical reading, in which God addresses man, hardly constitutes a prayer proper, the *shema'* has been surrounded by benedictions, by means of which it acquires fully liturgical character. The first one in the morning praises God for renewing the work of creation every day and, specifically, for making the sun rise and shine again, while in the evening it praises Him for bringing on the night. The second benediction gives thanks to God for having demonstrated his love for Israel, by choosing them from among the nations and giving them his Torah. The third, following after the *shema'*, opens with an affirmation of the truth of all that has been said in the Biblical passages and continues, apropos of Num. XV. 41, to give thanks for the redemption from Egypt. In the evenings there follows one more benediction of a petitionary character, requesting protection from all dangers at night; while in the morning the *'amidah* follows immediately.

VI. THE QEDUSHSHAH

Qedushshah, meaning sanctification, is the name given to a liturgical piece, based on Is. VI. 3 ('Holy, holy, holy, etc.') and Ez. III. 12 ('Blessed be the Glory of the Lord from his place'). These two verses are understood to contain the daily praise, proclaimed antiphonically by two separate angelic choirs. The description of these angelic praises is part of the first benediction preceding the morning *shema'* in all present-day rites; while in each repetition of the *'amidah*, in all communal services in which a quorum of at least ten worshippers participates, the *qedushshah* is added to the third benediction. Here a much augmented form is used, in which the prayer-leader opens with the declaration that we (i.e., the worshippers on earth) shall sanctify God in the manner of the angels on high following the two angelic verses, Israel joins in, as a third choir as it were, with Pd. cxlvi. 10 and in some versions (including the ancient Palestinian one) with the first verse of the *shema'*, to which God himself responds with 'I am the Lord, your God'.

Some form, at least, of the *qedushshah* was in vogue already by the second century C.E. There can be no doubt that this prayer originated in circles of mystics, who probably considered it a means of raising themselves up into the Heavens. While today the *qedushshah* is part of every service (except the evening service which lacks the repetition of the *'amidah*), in the old Palestinian rite it was limited to the morning services of Sabbaths and Festivals; on those occasions, however, the Palestinian liturgical poets made it the basis and the centre of gravity of most of their creations.

VII. THE QADDISH

In the present-day liturgy one of the most frequently used and most highly regarded prayers is the *qaddish* – an exalted hymn of praise, the beginning of which stresses eschatological motifs (which, in some versions are greatly emphasized and elaborated in detail): 'Glorified and sanctified be his great name throughout the world which he has created according to his will. May he establish his Kingdom . . .'. However, the *qaddish* was not part of the statutory synagogue prayers before the sixth century. Nevertheless, it is a very ancient prayer, but it was used originally not as part of the synagogue service but as a prayer of conclusion after the public sermon (cf. J. Heinemann in *JSS* V, 1960, p. 264f); this circumstance explains its Aramaic language and many curious features of style. Eventually, however, the *qaddish* came to be considered one of the mandatory parts of synagogue liturgy (even though it does not use the *berakhah*-formula); it is recited after each *'amidah* and also marks the transition between the various constituent parts of the service; it may be recited only when a quorum of ten is present. Latest of all is the use of the *qaddish* as the mourners' prayer; it may best be explained not as a prayer for the soul of the departed (which it definitely is not), but as a proclamation of faith on the part of the bereaved who thus 'justify the judgment' which has befallen them. As is well known, the *qaddish* recalls motifs and expressions prominent in Mt. VI. 9f. There is no need, however, to assume any direct influence, as similar themes and formulations occur in a variety of rabbinic prayers; they appear to have belonged to the 'common liturgical stock' of which the authors of various prayers would make use freely.

2 The Structure and Contents of Christian Liturgy

Clemens Thoma

I. STARTING POINT

THE liturgical crisis today concerns all Christian denominations. Sometimes it is suggested that a closer consideration of the Jewish liturgy, which has remained intact up to the present, might be of help to Christians in their distress. Access to Jewish sources is easier now than it was, because excellent expositions of the Jewish liturgy are now available for evaluation by Christians.[1]

There is also the fact that scholars are beginning to see that Christian liturgical studies in the past have been too exclusively concerned with work on Greek sources and late antiquity. Odo Casel, for example, dealt in his research chiefly with the New Testament and the Fathers, and hardly at all with the early Jewish liturgy.[2]

No one can seriously deny that a thorough investigation into the Jewish liturgy is now of pressing importance for Christian liturgical studies. But we should also realize that this is still an almost impossible task. We see at once that the Jewish liturgy is no more uniform than the Christian. There are not only the differences between the Sefardic and the Askenasian liturgies but countless local usages. There are huge linguistic and interpretative difficulties especially in the older Jewish liturgical texts in all their many forms. Moreover, among about 250,000 fragments discovered since 1896 in the Geniza of the Esra synagogue in Old Cairo there are many Jewish liturgical texts from late antiquity and the Middle Ages. Most of them have not yet been edited.[3] We must also take into account that there are liturgical problems in modern Judaism; nor is the Jewish liturgical scene a simple whole any longer. Changed religious and social conditions in the State of Israel, Europe and the USA are sharply increasing the demand for liturgical reform.[4] But Christian scholars of Judaism among others in European and American universities should apply themselves to intensive and systematic research into the difficult Jewish materials in the service of Christian liturgical scholarship.

In spite of all the difficulties and obscurities, it is still possible to set out differences and things in common between the Christian and Jewish liturgies and interpretations thereof. The Christian researcher must necessarily come to partly different conclusions from his Jewish partner – particularly in the matter of Christ's godhead.

II. DIFFERENCES AND SIMILARITIES

Several 'classic' differences between the Jewish and Christian liturgy prove on closer inspection to be entrenched apologetic positions, both Jewish and Christian. This is the case, for example, if we try to contrast the Jewish and Protestant services (service of the word of God) with the Catholic Mass (celebration of the mysteries). However, the Christian service, which is closest to the Jewish synagogue service, is not the Protestant service of the word but the traditional office of the Church sung in choir in monastic and priestly communities.

In both cases stress is put not only on the personal intentions of the individual praying but on the obedient performance of the office itself, which is an expression by official representatives of the consciousness of the whole community in prayer – all Israel or the whole Church. In both cases the service is composed of an interchange of hymns, psalms, responses, prayers of petition and praise, scripture readings and occasional ceremonial (bowing, small liturgical processions, and so on). Their purpose may be graphically clear, or quite obscure through historical accretions. Both services are not primarily concerned with the individual's approach to God in his daily religious life but with official representatives of the whole community offering praise to God. In this respect the Eastern Church appears to be closer to Judaism than the more pragmatic Western Churches.[5]

The 'mystery' side of Christian services also causes difficulties here. Many Jewish colleagues appear to see a sharp distinction between the 'mystery' and the Jewish synagogue services because they assume that the Christian Eucharist in particular is merely an adaptation of pagan mystery cults and sacrifices of late antiquity. It is extremely important to tell our Jewish brothers that this is not true. The Christian liturgy makes the mystery of salvation present and allows the congregation to take part in it; it is not an independent 'sacrifice' or an act of magic. The liturgy of the synagogue up to this day also contains similar elements of mystery. We do not mean only the Christian Eucharist and the Jewish Passaover feast and the Old Testament idea of *Zakar* (memorial)[6] but also the neglected aspect of the Old Testament early Jewish temple mysteries or special cults and the religious services of early Jewish apocalyptics.

Many ideas deriving from the temple mysteries and apocalyptic thought still have a strong influence on the modern synagogue service. In the Middle Ages and in early modern times the Jewish Cabbalists and Chassidim in particular brought about their incorporation into the common prayer service.[7] In late Old Testament times, the temple mystery cult saw the temple service as of cosmological, historical and notional religious importance. As in Jes. 6.1-6 the Temple was a place of mystical and cosmic importance, in which heaven, earth and the underworld, the beginning of time, the present and the end, Israel and the nations, coalesced. The ritually correct performance of the temple service brought the cult servants into mysterious communion with the greatest powers in the universe, God, the angels, the fathers of Israel and the coming salvation at the end of time. The Qumran sect and the Daniel and Enoch apocalyptics thought of themselves as chosen, secretly connected with the hosts of heaven and eventually with God in heavenly regions (cf. 1 QH III, 19-25; 1 QS XI, 2-9; Dan. 7; 1 En. 15, 8-15).[8] Such ideas also appear in *Qedusha* of the synagogue service and the Christian *Trishagion* or *Sanctus* of the traditional prefaces and elsewhere. Thus Judaism is not in a position to object to sacrament and mystery in the liturgy.

There are only two differences of crucial importance between the Jewish and Christian liturgies: Jesus Christ and the question of who officiates in the cult. The mysterious presence of Christ in his glory in the Eucharist is denied by Judaism. This means it must also deny the Christian view of the full eucharistic service given by Christ. Even in the pre-Christian parts of the Kaddish prayer, God is praised (see Neh. 9.5) in the words 'He the most high is above all blessing and all praise, all songs of praise and all the consolations that the world can utter'. This opposition cannot be minimized or argued away. Chrstian writers can merely mention that the New Testament and liturgical doxologies (cf. Rom. 11.33-36 and the final doxology if the Roman canon) and the 'classic' liturgical prayers are addressed to the 'Father' — that is the God of Israel — and not to Jesus Christ.

Judaism also denies the mediating power of the Christian priest. It cannot accept any of the Christian utterances in which the bishop, for example, symbolizes Christ or the unity of the Church in the liturgy. Even in Jesus' time the leader of the synagogue held a low position to which no form of ordination was attached. The higher Jewish offices in pharasaic and rabbinic Judaism (the patriarch, the Babylonian 'head of the diaspora', the professors and teachers) were not automatically connected with the celebration of the divine service, but with the exposition of Scripture, judgment in accordance with the Law, and the charitable and pastoral leadership of the community.[9] The synagogue service was and is an assembly of the laity. Jewish officials, including rabbis and the president of the community, are also present in a lay capacity. There is no priestly leadership or representation in a mystery rite.

Phenomenologically speaking, the Jewish service has four basic characteristics. It is praise of God (*berakhah*), directed to the will of God and for the consolidation of the community, and it is a daily prayer (*tesubah*).[10] That is the strength of Judaism. Christians should be able to learn from it instead of engaging in open or concealed attacks on the Jewish way of prayer.

Translated by Dinah Livingstone

Notes

1   Especially: I. Elbogen, *Der jüdische Gottesdienst in seiner geschichtlichen Entwicklung* (Hildesheim, 1962); J. Heinemann, *Prayer in the Period of the Tanna'im and the Amora* (Hebr., Jerusalem, 1966); S. R. Hirsch, *Israels Gebete* (Frankfurt, 1921); J. Maier, *Geschichte der jüdischen Religion* (Berlin, 1972); E. Munk, *Die Welt der Gebete* (Basle, 1962); J. Petuchowski, *Contributions to the Scientific Study of the Jewish Liturgy* (New York, 1970); F. Theiberger, *Jüdisches Fest, Jüdischer Brauch* (Berlin, 1967).
2   Cf. O. Casel, *Das Christliche Opfermysterium* (Graz, 1968).
3   Cf. J. Maier, 'Bedeutung und Erforschung der Kairoer "Geniza" ', *JAC* 13 (1970), pp. 48-61.
4   Cf. J. H. Petischowski, *Prayerbook Reform in Europe* (New York, 1969); J. Heinemann, 'Veränderungen im Gebetstext und in den Ordnungen des Synagogengottesdienstes, *Freiburger Rundbrief* 24 (1972), pp. 126-8.

5   R. Erni, *Das Christusbild der Ostkirche* (Lucerne, 1963).
6   Cf. H. Hang, *Das Opfer im AT* (Bibl. Beitr. I) (Einseideln, 1961), pp. 7-27.
7   G. Scholem, *Die jüdische Mystik in inhren Hauprströmungen* (Zürich, 1957); *ibid., Ursprung und Anfänge der Kabbala* (Berlin, 1962).
8   Cf. D. Flusser, 'Sanktus und Gloria', *Festschrift für O. Michel* (Leiden, 1963), pp. 129-52; J. Maier, *op. cit.*, note 2, pp. 30-4.
9   Cf. S. S. Cohon, *Authority in Judaism*, HUCA 11 (1936), pp. 595-646.
10   Cf. C. Thoma, 'Die Frömmigkeit im pharisäisch-rabbinischen Judentum', *Emuna* 7 (1972), pp. 324-30.

III Religiousness

1 Which Jew is a Good Jew?

Samuel Sandmel

TWO related developments — the age of rationalism beginning in the eighteenth century, and the sociological problems attendant on the decline or end of the ghetto in the nineteenth and twentieth centuries — raise the issue of defining what is a good Jew.

The definition was not difficult in the medieval ghetto. There and then a good Jew was one who conformed with the 'mitzvah' system which characterized all aspects of Jewish life: Sephardi ('Spanish') and Ashkenazic ('Germanic'), and Hassidim ('the pious'), and their adversaries the Mitnagdim ('opponents').

Mitzvah means commandment. The Jewish tradition included a recorded tabulation of these commandments, resulting in the figure of 613. Of this number, 365 were prohibitions and 248 — supposedly equivalent to the number of bones in the human body — were positive injunctions. The figure of 613 had arisen out of the ancient rabbinic interpretation of Scripture.

I. INTERPRETATION OF THE BIBLE

Sometimes Christians, especially Protestants, have some difficulty in grasping the role of Bible and ancient rabbinic *halaka* 'rabbinic requirements'). Perhaps a historical explanation can lead best into a proper understanding: In the year 70, the Romans destroyed the Temple in Jerusalem, thereby terminating for all time the sacrificial system enjoined in the Pentateuch, and virtually ending the role of the *cohen* ('priest'). On the one hand, scriptural requirements relating to Temple, sacrifice, and officiating priests were no longer viable, yet, on the other hand, the authority of Scripture was regarded as unabated.

How did they reconcile scriptural demands with the reality of the impossibility of fulfilling them? The way out was that of *interpretation*. Specifically, the view arose among the ancient rabbis, around the year 90, that prayer was an adequate surrogate for animal sacrifices. Worship in that unique institution, the synagogue, followed scrupulously the pattern of the defunct Temple service. Thus, in the Temple, sacrifices had been offered three times daily, morning, late afternoon and evening; hence, in the synagogue three prayer periods were mandatory, morning, late afternoon, and evening. These changes acknowledged the continuing authority of Scripture, but were a means of directing fidelity into new forms.

This sort of reconcilation spread into other areas beyond worship. Hence, the unfolding Jewish tradition slowly came to rest not precisely on Scripture itself, in a literal sense, but rather on Scripture as reinterpretated under the new conditions and new needs. To labour the point, animal sacrifice was no longer an operative mitzvah, but regular prayer was; the mitzvah system, though ultimately grounded in Scripture, was now actually only remotely scriptural. Indeed, in Judaism, scriptural literalism (of course, not at all in the modern sense of Christian fundamentalism) disappeared; the Jewish Bible was simply the Bible as mediated through its interpretation by the ancient rabbis and their successors.

This mediation has been known among Jews as the Torah *she-be al pe* ('Oral Law'), in contradistinction to the Scripture, the written Torah. The Oral Law, though, became recorded, in the Mishna and Gemara and in the Midrashim.

Mishna is a compilation of rabbinic law arranged on topics. Gemara is an elucidation (explanatory or legalistic determinative) of ambiguities or other unresolved elements of the Mishna. The Mishna was compiled, out of older oral materials, about 175. The Gemara was compiled to two 'redactions'. That which arose in Palestine in 450 did not gain the universal authority which the Babylonian version of 500 attained.

While analytically one could distinguish between a biblical law and a rabbinic substitution or elaboration of the Bible, for all practical purposes there was no compelling distinction; the mitzvah system was the entire array of the accumulated obligations.

Let it be recalled that scriptural law includes elements we might regard as civil, such as rules about theft and burglary, or manslaughter and murder, or inheritance or real estate. Rabbinic law accordingly, dealt with all aspects of life. In medieval civilization Jews ordinarily were accorded the rights of self-government, and hence they lived under Jewish rather than under state law. When the medieval ghetto began to fall, Jews in those parts of the world were often accorded the rights of citizenship, and thereafter made subject to state law.

II. THE QUESTION OF AUTHORITY

From the standpoint of Jews, could the state laws supersede Jewish laws? If practically they could and did, how about theoretically? To ask this in another way, could Jewish laws be deliberately terminated, or amended, from within Judaism on a traditionally sound basis?

The answer entails one of the great distinctions between Christian and Jewish theory. Christendom, in terms of an organized, monarchical clergy, has had a theory of authorized persons (who possess 'apostolic succession'). Such a clergy, in convention assembled, as at Nicaea or Chalcedon, could make decisions binding on the communicants. One might perhaps suggest this formulation, that in Christendom there have been, and are, individuals, or aggregates of them, who have been not only authorities *within* the tradition, but also, in a real sense, authorities *over* the traditiom.

Judaism never developed any such theory about authorized persons. It never explained the jurisdiction of certain eminent individuals whose personal attainments gained for them some sense of personal authority; where this latter happened, it was a matter of someone's local or regional influence. Whatever personal authority such an eminent rabbi might have gained, he could not ordinarily transmit that authority to anyone else. In sum, authority in Judaism has lain in what the inherited ancient books say, and not in any person. Jews have had neither popes nor ecumenical councils.

Such a situation has constituted a grand *cul de sac*, for it has meant that no person has the authority to alter, amend, or remove anything that has chanced to be recorded in the ancient books. When strict traditionalists have been willing to recognize and concede that some alterations have been desirable or even necessary, the next statement has been, 'but no one has the authority to make the change'. As happens in old religions, the only admissible alterations have involved an increase, whether of severity or rigour, but never a loosening or an abrogation. An old religious tradition accumulates; some things may of themselves fall into disuse, but these are seldom deliberately dropped.

In medieval situations, a good Jew was one who observed the totality of the accumulation of mitzvot, with fidelity and precision, and with scrupulous regard for all the minutiae. When the first perceptions arose that modern rationalism and changed sociological conditions implied that some deliberate alteration was necessary or desirable, the debate, which is still unended, began. The advocates of change have asserted that Judaism needed to adjust to the modern world, and ultra-traditionalists that it is the world which must adjust to Judaism, not

Judaism to the world.

Suppose that some individual Jew, in the Netherlands or in the Americas, wanted or needed to travel on some itinerary in which neither the rabbinic laws about kosher food, nor the attendant laws about the pots and the dishes, could be observed. He could either elect to forgo the trip, or else to ignore (and break) these food laws. These were his only choices, for the reason that there was no one who was authorized to tell such a Jew to follow his common sense, or to observe as much as he could in lieu of observing everything.

Where the situation exists that there is no authorized person, then every person tends to become his own authority.

III. DIFFERENT TENDENCIES

In the modern world, Jews with unquestioned Jewish loyalties found themselves breaking Jewish laws. (Some of them began to distinguish, as did second-century Christians, between the ethical laws as still valid, and the ceremonial as no longer so!) By medieval norms, such a 'law-breaker' could scarcely be a good Jew.

Reform Judaism is often deemed to have begun in 1806 when one Israel Jacobson introduced an organ into a Jewish chapel at Seesen. Reform was a by-product of the age of rationalism; it was indirectly a deliberate device which, by eliminating the 'exotic' elements in Jewish worship, might persuade German anti-Semites to desist from barring German Jews from their desired goal of citizenship. It needs to be noticed that 'Reformers' first instituted their changes and only thereafter did they try to give a reasoned justification for them. When the justificiations arose, they were a combination of rationalism and of historical scholarship. In clarification of the latter, it might seem obvious to the disengaged person that there was a time before the ancient rabbis existed, and hence their emergence into Judaism can be allocated to time and place. The ancient rabbinic laws involved innovation (at least to the view of a disengaged person). But from within Judaism the theory of an 'Oral Law' supposed that Moses had revealed the Written and the Oral Law simultaneously; hence, all items in the Oral Law were traceable to him, and therefore they entailed no innovation, and were in no sense a product of an age considerably later than Moses! (Christians have, somewhat similarly, pursued the crotchet of denying that there is ever anything innovative in an innovation.) Traditional Judaism, rich as has been its scholarship, seldom pursued strict historical study, or developed any keen sense of historical developments. Reformers, on the other hand, began to pursue historical scholarship as a means of justifying their alternations, by pointing to the fact of alternation and innovation in the previous ages, such as the time of the ancient rabbis.

Once such testimony of history was appealed to so that Reformers could justify the dropping of supposedly outmoded ceremonies and practices, and the additional step was taken of terming some ceremonies and practices irrational, or expressive of untenable religious ideas, or lacking aesthetic appeal. By and large Reformers were those who, impelled by religious emotion and Jewish fidelity, sought to fashion a 'modern' version of Judaism. Other Jews of the early nineteenth century followed Christians of the time in rejecting religion, whether the inherited, unchanged version or the new modifications. Sociologically, most such Jews, however 'bad Jews' they were, were self-consciously Jewish, loyally Jewish, and fully as much the victims of anti-Semitic limitations, economic and social, as were the most observant of the 'good' Jews. Thus, in example, Jewish socialism arose in the 1840s, in despair that western socialism would ever be solicitous about Jews. Jewish nationalism, despite the religious roots of Zionism, was essentially a secular imitation of the western nationalisms in which there seemed no legitimate or secure place for Jews. Jews, as it were, could lose their religion, but not their Jewish identity.

There is no occasion here to trace the vicissitudes of the experience of Jews in the nineteenth and twentieth centuries. Christian persecution ceased; 'racial' anti-Semitism was born. Jews migrated by the hundreds of thousands from the ghettoes of eastern Europe, both into western Europe and, in greater numbers, into the Americas, especially the United States. Jewish nationalism underwent an ebb and flow (and denunciation by westernized Jews). Hitlerism, and the indifference of western democracies to the plight of Jews, resulted in the Jewish conviction that only Palestine was a refuge of any consequence. The State of Israel was born in 1948.

From the standpoint of religious fidelity, our age is marked by some gradations with traditionalism, so that one needs to differentiate between *traditionalists* and *ultra-traditionalists* (such as the *hassidim* of Meah Shearim in Jerusalen). At the other extreme are the *Reform* or *Liberal Jews*, of whom some are extreme non-ceremonialists and others are adherents of broad aspects of traditionalism. In between as in the United States, are the Conservative Jews, who are more traditional than most Liberal-Reform Jews, but less traditional than the usual Orthodox Jews. But, in truth, these distinctions have become quite fluid; in the United States, often the difference is in the character of the synagogue worship, whether Orthodox, Conservative, or Reform, and not in the quantity or quality of one's personal observance of the mitzvah system. By and large in the United States, Orthodox, Conservative and Reform Jews all live alike, few of them in strict fidelity to the mitzvah system.

But an additional truth is that synagogue membership is, in the paradoxes of Jewish life, primarily a fiscal relationship, or else a quasi-phil-anthropic gesture, and not in itself a proof of, or, to be fair, a proclamation of piety. Most Jews in our day, being an urban people, are as pious in a Jewish way as are urban people of Christian origin in a Christian way. Synagogues are almost as empty as churches, and would be just as empty were all external pressures on Jews suddenly removed, and sociological peculiarities made to vanish.

Jewish loyalty, though, is quite another matter. When Hitler destroyed Polish Jews, American Jews felt a sympathetic pain. When Tunisian Jews reached the safety (?) of the State of Israel, American Jews joined in the breathing of a sigh of relief. We Jews shivered when the Rosenbergs were executed as atomic spies; we Jews have gloried in Kissinger's finding a way for the United States to get out of Viet Nam.

We Jews often prescribe for each other. Zionists have tried to define a good Jew as one who is a pro-Zionist, and as a bad Jew one who was (or now is) worried about Israel's future. Some Israelis have defined a good Jew as one who settles in Israel, and a bad Jew as one who does not. (Israelis usually soft-pedal this latter *vis-à-vis* American Jews.) American Jews have included a minority who have defined a good Jew as an anti-Zionist and a bad Jew as a Zionist. Most of us do the human thing and regard ourselves as the norm of goodness, and we assess others by ourselves.

What is a good Jew, I really do not know. My own inclination, since I shun using myself as a norm, is to suppose that a good Jew has some reasonably good education in Judaism; he has some sense of religious perspective, and some religious loyalty. He certainly needs to give of his possessions and of his personal services to charity. He ought to be a good citizen of the city and the country where he dwells (in my view, he need not personally migrate to Israel). He ought to be free of all bias, whether of race or religion, for a loyalty to Jews and Judaism is not enhanced by a denigration of other peoples or other faiths.

I would add that a good Jew wants to transmit and perpetuate Judaism. There are to my knowledge many worthy Jews who in this sense are bad Jews. To them Jewishness is a mere accident, and the values which I see in Judaism escape their notice, and, of course, their wish to preserve it.

I believe that I personally have some concerns that are different from my Jewish ones. In my case, it is higher education in general. In my case, it is a disproportionate love of symphonic and chamber music. I would be untrue to myself if I ignored these; I deplore it that Jews of culture and education often have little or no sense of personal relationship to chess or ballroom dancing.

In my view, one can be a worthy person and a 'bad' Jew. But I am personally not ready to call an unworthy person a good Jew, no matter how scrupulously he observes the mitzvot.

2 Which Christian is a Good Christian?

Jan Milic Lochman

I. CHRISTIANS WITHOUT UNIFORMS

IT has become more difficult for us today to give a clear and discerning answer to the question 'Which Christian is a good Christian?' Once it seemed simpler. The Churches' positions, both within and in relation to the world around them, were clearer. One knew — above all in the Catholic Church — who was a good Christian. There were safe criteria to judge by: on the theoretical side there was complete agreement about the traditions which the Church interpreted and ordered into a set of rules; in practice, the obvious appeal of ecclesiastically-projected cultural forms and organized religious devotions. In the Protestant Church, because of the already numerous denominations, a corresponding distinction is more difficult. Nevertheless it is to some extent perceptible. In the 'hard core' of Protestant orthodoxy particularly clear definitions and certainties were striven after. Here, in what can be described as the Puritan wing of the Reformation, characteristics of the moral and bourgeois life-style (understood chiefly in the sense of an 'interior secular ascetism') played an important role.

Of course in Christian theology the 'eschatological proviso' *vis-à-vis* all these far too rigid certainties about the 'Christian paradox' was not completely forgotten. It was admitted that a good Christian, even with an intrinsically Christian society, was an exception, a *rara avis* (Luther). And it was acknowledged that our ultimate justification depended solely on the judgment of God. But, supported by the traditional set of rules, people don't let this bother them. It was known already what a good Christian looked or should look like. The soldiers of Christ wore uniforms.

Today the situation is different. There have been changes within and without. This happened under external pressure, under the onslaught of the multiform secularization of modern life, above all in the traditional

50

Christian countries. But these changes also have another 'inner' dimension: the self-critical examination of belief. One has only to think of the profound changes in Catholic theology and the Catholic Church alone since the second Vatican Council, but also of similar changes in the Protestant and Eastern Orthodox Churches. In this fluid situation seen from within and without, some of the traditional roles are shown to be inappropriate and untenable. The primary characteristics of a good Christian life have been largely called in question.

These developments are not without dangers for Christian theology and not without painful symptoms in Church life. In the headlines of change theologians can very easily lose their 'theological heads' and fall victim to an unthinking relativism or reductionism. Many Christians have succumbed to uncertainty and indecisiveness. They are no longer certain what Christianity really means or what is permitted in the Church.

It would be foolish to ignore these dangers and to take the human need of the Church lightly. But it would be stupid too to underestimate the spiritual possibilities of the situation. I speak from my experience as a theologian from Eastern Europe. It was fortunate to be able to learn that the painful process undergone by the Churches in a Marxist society could have not only a harsh but a chastening and indeed enlightening effect on them. The credibility of the Christian life was not shattered but on the contrary deepened — not automatically to be sure but wherever the demands made of Christians were experienced not as misfortune but as a spiritual challenge.

This salutary experience is, I am sure, valid for other countries and situations; in other words, for the problematic contexts of the question: Who is a good Christian? It is possible that where the superficial answers are no longer so plain and universally accessible, a way could be revealed which might lead to the sources of Christian belief: the way from Rome or Geneva, not to Babylon but to Jerusalem. An encounter with the Bible has never harmed any Christian — even when it involved a few upheavals in established certainties and assurances.

II. HIDDEN IDENTITY

A meeting with the New Testament, above all with Jesus in the Gospels, soon shows that in that perspective especially it is difficult to give a clear or even an assured answer to the question of what a good Christian life really is. A remarkable reserve is already apparent in regard even to the epithet 'good'. I shall recall merely Jesus' meeting with the sympathetic 'rich young man' (Mark 10. 17ff), a scene which is particularly important for the question under examination. There Jesus refuses to apply the value-judgment 'good' to his own or indeed to any other person, with the argument that 'no one is good but only God'. The punch-line of the pericope only refines the problem. Of course it is good to keep the commandments. Jesus 'loved' when he remarked the young man's enthusiasm in this regard. And yet that isn't enough to win eternal life, to be a 'good Christian'; 'One thing you lack: go your way, sell whatever you have and give to the poor and you will have treasure in heaven,' (Mark 10.21). And that means 'being' is not to be derived from 'having' in the material and in the spiritual sense.

This theme is among those most typical of the New Testament — in the life of Jesus and in the preaching of the Apostles. One has only to think of Jesus' activity: it is always characterized by Jesus' acknowledgment of his orientation to the poor, to the people. He acknowledges his solidarity with the outcasts and the underprivileged. He eats and drinks with tax-gatherers and sinners. He prefers the company of those who, according to the valid religious and cultural norms of the day, were drop-outs and deviants. On the other hand the Gospels give the rich and the righteous a pretty bad press. Jesus is always colliding with them.

The Apostles take this line further and interpret is as the central decision of faith: our righteousness is the righteousness of *God. We* do not have to show any merit before God. The works of the law, traditional values, those religious and spiritual privileges inherited from our forefathers or acquired by our own responsibility — none of that suffices to justify us in the sight of God. No uniform makes a man into a 'good Christian'. Jews, pagans and Christians possess no 'racially innate' renown. The right of our life is that which is 'acquired' exclusively from God, or better: that right 'incurred' by him in the cross of Jesus and made our own: *sola fide, sola gratia.*

That is the context in which the question of what being a good Christian is has to be put if we are to understand it in the sense of the New Testament. But that means its extreme radicalization. To what extent? Ultimately what we are doing when we ask this question is to inquire into the true and authentic nature of Christian existence. In the main perspective of the New Testament, precisely this question recedes from the foreground of understanding, of direct comprehension. It is taken out of our hands and placed at God's discretion. As Christians we are not masters of our own identity; we are not religious virtuosos in sovereign command of their Christian existence and therefore able to orientate themselves unambiguously. Hence the Apostles refer to the history of God in the Old Testament but above all to the history of Christ where the justice, the salvation and, in this sense, the nature of their Christian existence are brought into question. *Christ* is 'our life' which 'is hidden with Christ in God' (Col. 1.3ff).

Martin Luther expressed with exceptional clarity this fundamental condition and basic structure of Christian life, when, for instance, he stressed in his commentary of Galatians: 'That is our basis; the Gospel orders us not to seize on good works and our perfection but the God of promise himself – Christ the mediator himself . . . And that is the way in which our theology is granted certainty: because it tears us from ourselves and places us outside ourselves, so that we do not support ourselves by our own powers, conscience, experience, individuality, works, but on what lies outside us: that is the promise and truth of God which cannot deceive' (*WA* 40.1, p. 583). This citation states formally what turn out to be decisive possibilities for answering the question of what a good Christian is. A good Christian is the man for whom his own being good is never the main concern of his own religiousness: instead he tries to live in the spirit of true *metanoia* while being turned towards God and his neighbours. He is the man who does not seek after his own righteousness but the righteousness of the kingdom of God. He is the man whose piety is not spent in the practice of Christian achievements and values but who is ready when necessary to discard all Christian 'uniforms' – 'in order to win Christ' (Phil. 3.5f).

III. FORGING AHEAD

Nevertheless we have not yet answered the question 'who is really a good Christian?' On the contrary. You could ask rather sceptically after reading the above: When you say so firmly that our identity is hidden with Christ in God, don't you push the Christian life into absolutely imperceptible, mystical spheres situated in the beyond? And doesn't that remove any duty or attachment to ordinary everyday Christian life? What then are members of other religions and philosophies to make of Christians? Are witness and dialogue and meaningful practice at all possible if the foregoing assumptions are taken into account?

In answer I should like to cite a well-known sentence of Nietzsche's: 'There was only one Christian and he died on the cross' (*The Anti-Christ*, art. 13). That was Nietzsche's sentence of death on Christianity. He denied Christians as they had developed in history any legitimate succession, any Christian identity, in regard to this One Christian. Christianity was still-born from the start.

With that assertion Nietzsche passed quite consciously over the central statement of the New Testament: that ultimately the history of the Man who was crucified did not end with his death, but had its new beginning – the Resurrection – in that death. Surely in the apostolic proclamation everything is unambiguously concentrated on the one name and destiny of the Crucified: on Jesus of Nazareth. The New Testament leaves no room for ambiguity: 'If Christ be not raised, your faith is in vain' (I Cor. 15.17). But he is risen from the dead, and that is the apostolic profession, the identity of Christian existence is thus eschatologically possible, and is historically assured. For the resurrected Christ is no spectre but the Jew from Nazareth who was known beforehand to his fellow men who bore witness to him. His actual history doesn't finish with the eschatological process of resurrection but is taken up again in real life. Therefore the words and actions of Jesus — even in the pneumatic enthusiasm of the first generation of Christians — were not forgotten but handed on and collected. They retain their directive and binding character. In short: the salvation of Christians is the salvation of God — but salvation within this human face.

In this perspective of the earthly history of Jesus of Nazareth the question of what a good Christian life really is is taken out of the area of the unobjective and imperceptible. It implies a visible succession to the visible history of Jesus. It points to the perceptible, earthly, mundane and ethical, and indeed the political aspects of existence.

Therefore the 'praxis of Jesus' is important — his creative freedom in which he places himself above all limits, prejudices and established conditions — not out of sectarian resentment or anarchistic antinomianism, but in order to reach his marginal, outcast and heavily-laden fellow men and to bring them into the operative sphere of the unconditional love of God. This practical life of Jesus is the directive force of an authentically Christian life: not in the sense of a programme and law to be observed and initiated, but as an initiative to commit oneself as a follower of Jesus in the struggle for ever-greater righteousness. Hence the question of the true nature of the Christian life must prove itself and be evaluated ethically and politically at the same time.

It appears that this emphasis in our Church and in the ecumenical movement is acknowledged to be more pronounced and more firmly stated than was previously the case. Much of this development is already quite public: Isn't the Church involving itself in secular affairs? Hasn't it lost her purely spiritual character? This question must be asked again and again in new situations. And yet this historical and social orientation is authorized and fundamental: in the Church's compassionate solidarity with the fate of the poor and oppressed. It is not here, where Christians involve themselves in the human world, that their identity as Christians is threatened. On the contrary, that happens only where we piously shield ourselves from 'secular affairs'. For such an attitude is untrue to the very nature of the Christ-event, which inseparably conjoins the eschatological and historical dimensions in witness to the resurrected and crucified Jesus.

In view of this background of eschatological Christian history the question 'which Christian is a good Christian' must be answered in terms of the day-to-day life of Christians. Both these aspects must be taken into consideration here. The point of *eschatological* history is that a 'good Christian' lives in the context of grace: he lives for God not for himself; he doesn't therefore need to play at being a hero. And above all he is no 'better' than Jews or atheists; they, Christians and all human beings, are in the same situation. But it is a matter of history: a 'good Christian' tries to live, in a spirit of renewal, in accordance with the divine grace articulated in the life and suffering of Jesus, in his own life, and therefore his own life-history, and that of his fellow men — 'In the liberty wherewith Christ hath made us free' (Gal. 5.1).

IV. A GOOD CHRISTIAN NEEDS GOOD JEWS

Has the question about good Christians anything to do with the relationship between Christians and Jews? I am convinced that it has and indeed in both its implications. A good Christian takes his point of reference from the grace of God and can therefore never forget that he is similarly linked to the God of Abraham, Isaac and Jacob. There is for him as for Jesus no other God. And there is therefore in this last analysis no 'other people' — no other community of believers with whom he would be so closely bound, as with the Jews. A good Christian cannot, for this most fundamental reason, be anti-Semitic — a statement which of course must imply a highly critical and self-critical inquiry into Christian history and the present day.

And the other implication: the obvious moral and political dimension of being a good Christian is inconceivable without an encounter with the religion of the Jews, and above all with the Book of Israel, with the Old Testament. The history that Jesus wove, pointing the way forward to the people of Israel, is without them, incomprehensible and unbinding. The Church has that ever-continuing experience; without the Fathers of Israel and the prophets, Christianity sinks — and with it Christians — into pagan mythology.

So a good Christian needs good Jews. And perhaps also a good Jew needs good Christians.

Translated by M. Carol

IV Messianic Hope

1 In Judaism

Jakob Petuchowski

I. THE TWO BIBLICAL NOTIONS OF REDEMPTION

IF the world is the handiwork of God, and if the world does not turn out to be as 'very good' as, according to Genesis, it was intended to be, then it would follow that what is now only potentially 'very good' must one day, become 'very good' in actuality.

Again, if the One God of Israel is, at the present time, not universally acknowledged as the God of all mankind, and if his moral law governing the relationships among men as yet falls short of unanimous acceptance, then — in view of the fact that he himself has written the script of mankind's drama — it would stand to reason that the day will surely come on which he will be so acknowledged. And, with this acknowledgment, there will come the universal acceptance of his Law. Nations will 'flow unto the mountain of the Lord', accept the Torah which comes from Zion, and proceed to 'beat their swords into ploughshares and their spears into pruning-hooks'. (Is. 2.2-4.)

Again, the covenant which God made with Israel has as one of its most prominent clauses Israel's title to the Land of Israel. Yet, in actual historical fact, Israel has been anything but a nation in peaceful and undisputed possession of its own soil. But, since the covenant is eternal, it follows that the day must come on which God will make good on this clause of his contract.

Such is the type of explicit and implicit reasoning which, in the biblical period, led to the positing of messianic redemption as one of the major three affirmations of biblical religion — the other two being creation and redemption.

But there is no uniform way in which the Bible describes the occurrence of that redemption. In fact, the Rabbis, who inherited the Bible, and who looked upon it as a unified whole, had to come to terms with two biblical notions of redemption which appear to be contradictory. On the one hand, there are biblical passages which create the impression that redemption is a process in which man is very much involved. As man becomes more moral and obedient, as social justice becomes increasingly rectified, and as the rulers become more attuned to the word of God, the fulfiment of history, the End of Days, will be brought about.

On the other hand, the Book of Daniel — prototypical of apocalyptic literature — operates with quite a different concept. The 'Kingdom of the saints of the Most High' will burst miraculously — vertically, as it were — into the normal course of history, and bring history, as we know it, to a predetermined End. Since that End is predetermined by God, there would seem to be little that man can do, one way or another, to bring it about. At best, man might attempt, on the basis of mysterious and mystifying hints, to figure out and calculate just when that apocalyptic End is going to burst in on us.

No doubt, there were Rabbis in the classical period of Rabbinic Judaism who championed the one biblical position, and Rabbis who championed the other. Joseph Klausner, in his *The Messianic Idea in Israel*, has endeavoured to show how political circumstances were responsible for bringing one point of view to the fore at one time, and another point of view at another time. For example, as long as there was hope in armed rebellion against Rome — as under Bar Kokhba — the messianic idea reckoned with man's active participation. When the Bar Kokhba rebellion against Rome failed, belief in man's ability to bring about his own salvation gave way to the belief in God's miraculous intervention.

II. ATTEMPTS AT HARMONY

Yet, over and above this linking of the messianic idea to the changing political fortunes of the nation, there is discernible a more general attempt on the part of the Rabbis to reconcile and to harmonize the two inherited and contradictory biblical notions. That is to say, the Rabbis both accepted the notion of a predetermined End, and, at the same time, they refused to give up man's share in helping to bring it about.

On the verse in Isaiah 60.22 ('I the Lord will hasten it in its time.'), Rabbi Joshua ben Levi (third century C.E.) made the following comment: 'If Israel merits it, "I will hasten it." If Israel does not merit it, it will be "in its — predetermined — time." ' (B. *Sanhedrin* 98a.)

The assumption here is that the predetermined End is far off in the distant future, but that, by means of meritorious acts, Israel might persuade God to bring about the End much earlier than originally scheduled.

Similarly, Rabh (third century C.E.), without denying that there was such a thing as a Danielic End, insisted that 'all the dates calculated for such an End had already gone by'. The End just did not happen – no doubt, because man was in no fit spiritual state to experience it. But, with the calculated times for the End gone by, the promised messianic fulfilment now depends exclusively on man's 'repentance and good deeds'. (B. *Sanhedrin* 97b.)

It was in this manner that some of the leading Rabbis tried to do justice to both Isaish and to Daniel; and the attempt has remained paradigmatic for Rabbinic Judaism as a whole. The messianic fulfilment is the result of a joint endeavour of both God and man. Of course, there were times when God's part was emphasized more than man's part; and there were times when man's part was more emphasized than God's part. Thus, Gerson D. Cohen has shown in some detail how the Spanish and Portuguese Jews were more given to translating messianic speculation into political action than the French and German Jews of the Middle Ages.[1] But at no time prior to the nineteenth century was the question ever completely answered in terms of an 'either/or' formulation. It was always: 'Both!' God and man. The problem was only how much was each to contribute.

III. TWO TYPES OF SECULARIZED MESSIANIC HOPE

In the nineteenth century, two movements in modern Judaism were to break with that traditional formula. The two movements seemed at that time – and for a long time thereafter – to be absolutely antagonistic towards each other. But, as David Neumark pointed out as early as 1916, in his essay, 'Reform Judaism and Nationalism',[2] they really shared in the common endeavour of secularizing the messianic hope. Zionism did so by refusing to wait any longer for a Messiah sent by God to lead the Jews back to Palestine. The Jews were now going to get there under their own steam. Reform Judaism, as stated in the 'Pittsburgh Platform' of 1885, recognized 'in the modern era of universal culture of heart and intellect, the approaching of the realization of Israel's great Messianic hope for the establishment of the kingdom of truth, justice and peace among all men'.

(One might also mention Socialism as yet a third attempt at secularizing the Jewish messianic hope. But, while Zionism and Reform Judaism remained Jewish in cultural and religious terms, no such claim can be made for Socialism – except for a few specific and self-proclaimed

Jewish Socialist movements.)

Few, if any, would, in 1974, see in the beleaguered State of Israel a messianically redeemed enclave in an unredeemed world — although the State of Israel may indeed be a part, but only a part, of a universal redemptive process which may take a very long time to work itself out. And as for the 'modern era of universal culture of heart and intellect', in which the Reformers put all their trust, there is no denying the *intellect*. The destruction of six million Jews was a great scientific and technological achievement, which drew heavily on the trained German intellect. It was, however, the 'universal culture of heart' which did not seem to be quite forthcoming!

IV. THE INNER DIALECTICS OF JEWISH MESSIANISM

Perhaps, after all, man is incapable of pulling himself up by his own bootstraps without divine assistance. Considerations of this kind have led Steven S. Schwarzschild, some years ago, to argue for the restoration of the personal Messiah to the liturgy of Reform Judaism, a liturgy which long ago had substituted 'redemption' for the 'redeemer', and the 'messianic age' for the Messiah.[3] Schwarzschild, himself a social activist of pronounced leftist leanings, was, of course, far from arguing for human passivity. On the contrary, he pointed out that the very Rabbis, who spoke of the personal Messiah as God's part in messianic fulfilment, also stressed man's part in bringing that fulfilment about. While Schwarzschild's suggestion has not as yet been incorporated into the liturgy of American Reform Judaism, there is, nevertheless, a greater readiness now in Reform Jewish circles than there has been for a long time before to bring God back into the picture of messianic fulfilment.

After all, without a belief in God, one would not dabble in messianic speculation to begin with. There is no evidence for automatic progress in this world of ours. History, as the ancient Greeks thought, might just as well be cyclical — as the stock market indeed turns out to be. It is only because we believe in God, in the God of biblical revelation, that the concept of a messianic redemption of history arises in the first place. In other words, there is a greater readiness now, even in some Reform circles, to revert to the old rabbinic solution of 'both God and man', rather than settling for an 'either/or' alternative.

Much, of course, depends on what is meant by the 'End'. The nineteenth-century Reformers identified it with social meliorism and the spread of democracy. Among the ancient Prophets there were those who saw it primarily in a restoration of the Jewish people to Zion and Jerusalem. Other prophets were more universalistic. There would be universal peace and justice. As long as Israel can have its independent way of life, as long as 'every man can sit under his vine and under his fig-tree, with none to make him afraid', let all the nations, each walk in the name of its own god (Micah 4.4f). Still others seem to have thought in terms of a universal conversion to Hebrew ethical monotheism.

The Rabbis, heirs of *all* the biblical views on this subject, and often rising to lofty universalistic heights (witness, above all, the Rosh Hashanah liturgy, and the second paragraph of the *Alenu* prayer which concludes every Jewish worship service), were existentially concerned primarily with improvements in the fate of the Jews. So much so, in fact, that the Babylonian sage, Samuel (second-third centuries C.E.), could come up with the statement that 'the only difference between our present existence and the messianic age is that, in the latter, the Jews will no longer be subject to foreign domination' (B. *Berakhoth* 34b). He was echoed in this by the greatest Jew of the Middle Ages, Moses Maimonides (twelfth century). (*Hilkhoth Melakhim*, chapter 12.)

But Maimonides saw in the messianic fulfilment more than just the regaining of Jewish national independence. He also looked forward to full freedom for Torah study, the absence of famine, war, jealousy and competition, the presence of material abundance, and the striving of all mankind to know the Lord (*ibid*). It can be said that the messianic picture drawn by Maimonides pretty much sums up the Jewish messianic expectations through the millenia. Certainly, those were the criteria which Jews have always applied when judging the credentials of the various messianic claimants which, in the course of their long history, have arisen in their midst. Thus far, no one has met those criteria, and, from the Jewish point of view, the world remains pre-messianic, unredeemed.

Rabbi Yohanan, a Palestinian teacher of the third century C.E., said: 'The Son of David will come only in a generation that is either altogether righteous or altogether wicked.' (B. *Sanhedrin* 98a.) In that profound statement, he made allowance both for the Prophetic and the apocalyptic concept of the Messiah. The messianic age will either be the consequence of mankind's moral improvement, or it will come by a miraculous divine interference in the historical process, to save man from destroying himself. Since no generation thus far has considered itself either completely righteous or completely wicked, and since mankind is constantly veering between the two extremes, the messianic hope perpetually figures in new constellations; and a new dimension is forever added to the inner dialectics of Jewish messianism.

Notes

[1]   Gerson D. Cohen, 'Messianic Postures of Ashkenazim and Sephardim', in Max Kreutzberger, ed., *Studies of the Leo Baeck Institute* (New York, 1967),

pp. 117-56.
2   Reprinted in David Neumark, *Essays in Jewish Philosophy* (New York, 1929), pp. 91-100.
3   Steven S. Schwarzschild, 'The Personal Messiah – Towards the Restoration of a Discarded Doctrine', in *Judaism*, Vol. V (1956), pp. 123-35.

2 In Christianity

Jürgen Moltmann

I. 'ARE YOU HE WHO IS TO COME?'

THE messianic question about the 'one who is to come' shows the close kinship between Judaism and Christianity. The answers that each hears seem to show them irrevocably divided. 'The one who is to come' is a cipher concealing the identity of the promised Messiah and the expected Son of man.[1] The Messiah is the king of the last times who restores Israel and through Sion brings justice and peace to the nations. Christian scholars often describe him too narrowly as 'an exponent of Jewish national eschatology'.[2] According to Daniel 7 the Son of man is a pre-existent heavenly being. After the fall of the bestial world kingdoms he brings the universal kingdom 'of man' from God.[3] Scholars often make the Messiah responsible for historical redemption and the Son of man for redemption from history. In Jewish apocalyptic, however, the two symbols of hope were so firmly fused that a two-tier doctrine of the Messiah arose in which the Messiah represented the immanent side of the realization of the kingdom of God and the Son of man its transcendent side.[4] Both symbols of hope, however, are schematic and lack identifiable detail, for they must be transparent of him whose future they are meant to mediate. The cipher of the 'coming one' was also applied in prophecy to God himself, as in Isaiah 35.4-5: 'God himself will come and save you. Then the eyes of the blind shall be opened, and the ears of the deaf unstopped; then shall the lame man leap like a hart, and the tongue of the dumb sing for joy.'

The enquiry about the 'coming one' was put by the Jews to Jesus of Nazareth. According to Matt. 11.4, his answer was indirect: 'Go and tell John what you hear and see: the blind receive their sight and the lame walk, lepers are cleansed and the deaf hear, and the dead are raised up and the poor have the good news preached to them.' Luke sums up the mission of Jesus as the fulfilment of the promise of Is. 61.1-2: 'to preach good news to the poor . . . to proclaim release to the captives and recovering of sight to the blind, to set at liberty those who are oppressed, to proclaim the acceptable year of the Lord' (4.18-19). The liberations which take place through the action and preaching of Jesus speak for him. They are signs of the messianic age. To those who experience and believe in them, he reveals himself as 'the one who is to come'.[5] Jesus' answer to the Baptist's question is indirect because awareness of the messianic time depends on faith. But Jesus connects the awakening of this messianic faith with his human person and his sufferings: 'blessed is he who takes no offence at me'. The question, 'Are you he who is to come, or shall we look for another?' is thus returned to the liberating experience of sufferers with Jesus, and their faith.

II. JEWISH OBJECTIONS

The objections of those who 'look for another' begin here. 'The Jew has a keen sense of the world's lack of redemption, and within this absence of redemption he recognises no enclaves of redemption. The idea of a redeemed soul within an unredeemed world is essentially, basically alien to him; the primordial ground of his existence makes it inadmissible. This is the heart of Jesus' rejection by Israel, not in a merely external, merely national understanding of messianism.'[6] As a comment on later Church doctrine, this may be correct, but did the poor to whom he preached the good news, the sick he healed or the outcasts he accepted regard themselves as 'redeemed souls' in an unredeemed world? 'Judaism in every shape and form has always maintained a concept of redemption which it treated as a process taking place in the public world, on the stage of history and in the context of a community, in short, definitely taking place in the visible world . . . In contrast, there is in Christianity a view which treats redemption as a process in the spiritual and invisible realm, unfolding in the soul and the world of each individual and bringing about a secret transformation which need have no external correlate in the world . . . The reinterpretation of the prophetic promises of the Bible in terms of a realm of inwardness . . . was always regarded by the religious thinkers of Judaism as an illegitimate anticipation of something which could at best only appear as the interior of a process whose decisive elements took place in the external world and never without this process.'[7]

Was the original faith of the healed and the liberated really this sort of interiorization of salvation? It is true that in the history of Christianity the realistic messianic hope has often been replaced by spiritualizing and individualizing representations of salvation.[8] Not only Christianity, however, but Judaism, had to struggle in order to assert the realism and universalism of their hope in the face of gnosis. There cannot therefore be 'completely different concepts of redemption underlying the attitude to messianism in judaism and in Christianity'.[9] In my view the difference depends on the eschatological experience of time which takes place or does not take place in Jesus. The Baptists's question is the question about the messianic 'hour'. It is a 'temporal' question, but in addition what decides the validity of the hope which grows out of it is the form of the messianic anticipation of redemption in the still unredeemed world. Is it the Mosaic Torah or the gospel of Jesus? Who has the Torah on their side, and who has the Gospel? — In their dispute about the messiahship of Jesus Christianity and Judaism have grown far apart, to the detriment of both: 'For Jews the Messiah is in danger of disappearing into the kingdom of God, and for the Christian Church the kingdom of God is in danger of disappearing into the figure of the Messiah.'[10] A hope for the kingdom of God without a messianic present in history must lead to the expectation of a world catastrophe, because 'this world cannot support the righteousness of the kingdom'. On the other hand, a messianic present without a hope for the kingdom of God which is to fulfil it inevitably becomes an illusion and ignores the 'mystery of evil'. Christian Christology must stop making Judaism suspicious of the hope for the Messiah and the Jewish expectation of the kingdom must stop making Christians suspicious of an eschatology of the real future.

III. THE MESSIAH AS A FIGURE OF SUFFERING

Jewish teaching about the Messiah is not limited to revanchist or utopian hopes in 'the one who is to come' as the one who will either restore the 'life with the Fathers' or establish the new Jerusalem. The apocalyptic traditions also make the point that his coming cannot be calculated or deserved. He comes unexpectedly, and in the case of many when all hope has been extinguished in suffering. He also comes in concealment and may already be present unrecognized. Legend has him born on the day of the destruction of the Temple and in preparation for his Day wandering ever since unrecognized through all the nations of the earth. His primary shape is ultimately one of suffering. He lives among beggars and lepers. He suffers with the persecuted children of Israel. Similarly, the day of messianic liberation will be inaugurated by apocalyptic tribulations and the terrors of downfall. Recognition of the Messiahship of Jesus, not only in his mission and the signs and wonders which accompany it, but even more in his sufferings, his vulnerability and powerlessness and finally in his death as an outcast, is not a distinctive mark of Christianity, but one it shares with Judaism. Though there are few Jewish references to a suffering and dying Messiah, and none to one rejected by the Law, the Job figure of the Jewish people and its history of suffering sufficiently meets the description.[11]

The suffering and death of Jesus are treated by the Gospels as the suffering and death of 'the one who is to come' and therefore painted in apocalyptic colours. Because they regarded him as an eschatological person, the New Testament writers saw in his fate the anticipation of the last judgment. But if the judgment which is to fall on all has already been executed on this individual, he has suffered vicariously and for the benefit of all. Understanding Jesus' death in terms of the messianic categories in which it appeared and is understood in the light of Easter means regarding it as an act of suffering performed by the prevenient love of God for the 'dead'.[12]

Through the sufferings of the Messiah sufferers obtain messianic hope. Through the Messiah's self-giving those who have been 'given up' (Rom. 1.26) — Jews and Greeks — obtain the freedom to choose eternal life. Through his undergoing judgment *for them*, sinners are justified *in him*. This is why the Christian faith has regarded the impotent suffering death in abandonment of Jesus not as a refutation of his messianic hope, but as its deepest realization in the conditions of a Godless and inhuman world which stands under the coming judgment. That is why it has discovered the hope of sufferers in the sufferings of this one who was 'to come'. It has found the liberation of the guilty in the death of this innocent victim.

IV. MESSIANIC CHRISTOLOGY

Must the Christian faith cut off the Jewish Messiah figure from its connexions with the greater kingdom of God when it applies messianic language to Jesus? If the faith does this, it will be totally unable to tolerate any open Jewish hope alongside itself.[13] But if it does not do this, how can it hope in Jesus with any assurance? Jesus has 'unmistakeable and unforgettable traits, which is just what the Jewish image of the Messiah by its very nature cannot have. In it all personal characteristics can only be seen as completely abstract because it is not based on any lived experience'.[14] Does Jesus really possess these features? In fact his 'form' destroys the religious longing for hope to take a definite shape: 'He had no form or comeliness . . . as one from whom men hide their faces he was despised, and we esteemed him not', say the gospels along with Is. 53.

His 'personality' is defined by his fate: 'crucified and raised up', as the oldest creeds say. This indeed makes him unmistakeable and unforgettable, but his 'living experience' is also a 'deadly' one. The 'double result of his life' (M. Kahler) reveals the eschatological transcendence of God. He does not let himself be fixed in an image, but frees us from the images of idols of experience and hope to await the God who is to come. Because of this Christology cannot be the end of messianic eschatology. This euphoria of fulfilment has constantly deified Jesus and tried to destroy Jewish discontent. Instead, Christology must lead much more to open eschatological hope. The cross and resurrection leave their mark on the present and future in God's anticipatory action. Anyone who engages in uncontrolled anticipation here loses the future along with the present. An eschatology based on Christianity must therefore start from an eschatologically open Christology.[15] Christianity can only treat Jesus as the confirmation and fulfilment of the messianic hope if it discovers within this person the messianic future of God himself. Only when it recognizes the difference and the connexion between the rule of the Son of man and the rule of God himself can it recognize its own eschatological impermanence. The Pauline idea that the Son will hand over rule to the Father, so that God may be all in all (1 Cor. 15.28) points in this direction on the theological level. If it is taken seriously it means the end of Christian absolutism. The Church will see itself as provisionally final and hope, with the Jews and for the poor, for the completion of the kingdom in the history of God.

V. THE SUFFERINGS OF THOSE WHO HOPE
AND THE HOPE OF THOSE WHO SUFFER

I have examined the question of the Messiahship of Jesus in so much detail because there can be no new convergence between Christianity and Judaism without a revision of the Christological foundations of Christianity. Jewish criticisms of historical formations in Christianity are often accurate. We are now beginning to see, however, that these historical forms, the spirtualization and individualization of salvation and the deification of Jesus before his cross in a spirit of triumphalist clericalism cannot survive. Jewish criticisms must lead Christianity to a deeper and better understanding of Jesus, his mission, his sufferings and his future. But this means that the factual existence of the Jews is a constant question against the messianic hope in Christ. The presence of the Jews constantly forces Christians to see that they are not yet at their goal, and that their Church too is not the goal; instead, eschatological and also provisional, and in brotherly openness, they are still on the way.

Franz Rosenweig rightly said that the most profound reason for Christian hatred of the Jews was the hatred of Christians for themselves, 'hatred of their own imperfection, of their own falling short'.[16] But the more Christianity frees itself from clerical and political intoxication with fulfilment, the more it will be able to live with the messianic hope and recognize t..e permanent incompleteness of the Jewish hope for the Messiah. Intoxication with fulfilment without an acceptance of the cross was the fate of Christian triumphalism in the past. This temerity leads to resignation and the death of hope. The most important requirement to keep alive the messianic hope in Christianity is for the suffering Jesus and his fellowship with the outcasts to be brought into the foreground. Gershom Scholem records a 'truly powerful "rabbinic fable" of the second century': the Messiah will sit among the lepers and beggars at the gates of Rome. 'This symbolic contrast between the true Messiah sitting at the gates of Rome and the head of Christianity in power there accompanied the Jewish doctrine of the Messiah through the centuries.'[17] Will not those who 'beseech you, on behalf of Christ, be reconciled' (2 Cor. 5.20) one day be found among those whom the Son of man calls the least of his brethren (Matt. 25) and declares blessed?

The messianic hope which Jews and Christians received together but have experienced differently was given to them not for their benefit, but for abandoned humanity. Consequently the Messiah will not appear in Jerusalem, nor in Rome nor in Geneva. He will come among the poor, the mourners, those who hunger for righteousness and are persecuted for it. He will appear among the 'beggars and lepers' in Jerusalem, Rome, Geneva and other places. Only when the suffering of those who have the messianic hope becomes the hope of those who suffer in this world will Jews and Christians really understand their provisional finality and honour god-forsaken mankind's Messiah.

Translated by Francis McDonagh

Notes

1   S. Mowinkel, *He That Cometh. The Messianic Concept of the Old Testament and Later Judaism* (1956); G. Scholem, 'Zum Verständnis der messianischen Idee im Judentum', *Judaica* I (1963), pp. 7-74.

2   R. Bultmann, *Gluaben und Verstehen* II (1952), p. 242; P. Vielhauer, *Aufsätze zum Neuen Testament* (1965), pp. 55ff. and others.

3   P. Vielhauer, 'Jesus und der Menschensohn', *Aufsätze*, pp. 92ff.; J. M. Schmidt, *Die jüdische Apokalyptik* (1969).

4   Cf. the traditional formula used by Paul, Rom. 1.3, and Scholem, 'Messianische Idee', p. 21.

5   H. J. Iwand, *Die Gegenwart des Kommenden* (1957).

6   S. Ben-Chorin, *Die Antwort des Jona* (1956), p. 99.

7   Scholem, pp. 7-8; F. Rosenzweig, *Der Stern der Erlösung* (1954^3), III, pp. 97ff., 178-9.

8   R. Bultmann, *History and Eschatology* (1962) shows this, and is also an example of the process. Scholem, p. 74, rightly says, 'We may perhaps say that the messianic idea is the authentic anti-existentialist idea'.

9   Scholem, p. 7.

10   Ben-Chorin, *Die Antwort des Jona*, p. 5.

11   M. Susman, *Das Buch Hiob und das Schicksal des jüdischen Volkes* (1948^2).

12   J. Moltmann, *Der gekreuzigte Gott* (1973^2).

13   Cf. A. Schwarz-Bart, *Der Letzte der Gerechten* (1960).

14   Scholem, pp. 38-9.

15   Cf. Moltmann, *Theology of Hope* (London and Richmond, Va., 1969).

16   Rosenzweig, III, p. 197.

17   Scholem, p. 28.

V Jesus

1 To What Extent is Jesus a Question for the Jews?

David Flusser

I. DIFFICULTIES OF UNDERSTANDING

THE German writer G. E. Lessing was also a thinker. In 1780 he wrote a fragment called 'The Religion of Christ'. What he says is still worth reading today even though we may not agree with everything. Let us quote some of it: 'The religion of Christ and the Christian religion are two quite different things. The religion of Christ is the religion which he himself believed in and practised as a man . . . the Christian religion is that religion which holds that Christ was more than a man and as such makes Christ himself an object of worship. It is hard to see how both these religions, the religion of Christ and the Christian religion, can co-exist in Christ as one and the same person . . . At least it is obvious that the religion of Christ appears quite different in the Gospels from the Christian religion. The religion of Christ is contained in the clearest and simplest words; the Christian religion appears so uncertainly and ambiguously that there is hardly a single place in the Gospels about which two people have thought the same ever.'

These are hard words and not altogether true. But modern theology often does no better. It distinguishes between the historical Jesus and the kerygmatic Christ. Unlike Lessing, who professed the religion of Christ 'which every human being can hold with him in common', many modern theologians come down on the side of the kerygmatic Christ. If they believe in the resurrection of Jesus they should realize that there must at least be a personal unity between the Jesus who preached and the Risen Lord they preach.

But enough of that. I will not overstep the limits imposed on me by my Jewishness. But I would like to stress just one thing. In former disputes and in the Jewish-Christian dialogue of today the Jewish partner was more often obliged by circumstances than the Christian to stylize his position, as it were, and partly deny his own human nature. There are two reasons for this. First, it is not often sufficiently realized that the Jewish religion is pre-Christian: that is, an essentially non-Christian religion. The Christian is apt to think of the Jewish point of view as merely a non-Christian one which the Jew shares with other non-Christians. Of course I can understand the overwhelmingly liberating experience of realizing, for example, that one has been released from sinfulness by the blood of Christ. I also know that a Christian should treasure the grace of being given this good news in earliest childhood. As a child he did not receive this message with fear and trembling but as an obvious truth. How many of my Christian readers are certain that they would have come to believe in the un-self-evident paradox of the cross if they had been brought up as non-Christians? Would they have had the courage to give up their faith as adults? For the Old Testament is not so obvious that it leads to the cross of Christ.

If a Jew and a Christian want to understand one another in regard to Christology the Christian should remember he is talking to a non-Christian.

Secondly, the reason why circumstances often force a Jew in dialogue with Christians to deny a part of his human nature is connected with the spcific character of the Christian religion. Christianity is different from other religions in that it makes a confession of faith in a very particular object. 'If you confess with your lips that Jesus is Lord and believe in your heart that God raised him from the dead, you will be saved.' (Rom. 10.9.)

Christianity proclaims something which must be believed, and it is absolutely necessary for the will to make the act of faith. This often means a conscious one-sidedness which may be carried over into other matters. The Christian thinks he knows the goal or goals. Because the Christian must think in this one-sided way he demands that same kind of argument from his non-Christian partner, which means also from a Jew. But the Christian usually does not realize that the non-Christian does not feel obliged by his reglion always to have ready a Buddhist, Muslim or Jewish answer. The non-Christian does not feel that he betrays his religion when he sometimes has no answer or when he sometimes merely wants to be human. So what should we do when the question is put to us, as it is to me: to what extent is Jesus a question for *the Jews*? Must I play the dogmatic-keygmatic game, even though I am even less inclined than most Jewish speakers to engage in normative apologetic thinking?

II. RETURN TO JESUS?

Before I answer the actual question I would like to say one more thing. Jews facing a possible conversion are often told they must return to Jesus. I do not think this is a good way of putting it. For a Christian a return to Jesus means an act of faith, and I have already said a decision of the will to make such a confession is a specifically Christian phenomenon. Non-Christian Islam also finds such a notion hard to understand. For them Jesus is an important prophet and a judge, but the Moslems to not *confess* Jesus, neither to they confess Mohammed. The same is true for the Jews and Moses. Because the notion of a specifically Christian act of will professing faith is foreign to a Jew, with the best will in the world he can only relate to Jesus as he relates to Moses.

Sometimes the approach to the Jews takes the form of saying they should recognize Jesus as a *prophet* or even as the greatest prophet. This does not quite make sense to a Jew either. A Jew would not want to *confess* that Jesus was a prophet. He would ask whether there was evidence to show that Jesus belonged to the class of prophets. And even if the answer was Yes it would not be decisive for Judaism as a whole because Jesus lived after Old Testament times. Judaism would require a council to decide the issue, but there has never been an official body in Judaism to make dogmatic decisions. Even if every Jew accepted that Jesus was a prophet that would be the result of scholarly conviction and not an expression of faith.

The question to the Jews would be better expressed thus: Was Jesus the Messiah of the Jews or, rather, will he be the Messiah? For the Jews the question should be stated as about the future, as I think Jesus also would have stated it. No one feels more strongly than the Jews that the world today is a world of brutal injustice and not the messianic kingdom. Jews expect the Messiah to save our people and, in this darkness this is our hope for ourselves and for the world. If I am not mistaken it is a hope we share with the 'historical' Jesus. The idea that the Messiah frees those who believe in him from sin through his blood is an exclusively Christian one and not altogether a New Testament idea either. For according to the New Testament this salvation is not the *messianic* act of Jesus; the day of the Son of man is still to come. Moreover, many Christians object to the formulation of the question as whether Jesus was the Messiah of the Jews. Christianity quickly forgot the actual meaning of the term Messiah. Even in the New Testament the Greek term *Christos* (Messiah) is already becoming another name for Jesus. Many Christians today simply cannot conceive that the Christian idea was originally identical with that of the Old Testament prophets, namely that at the end Israel and believers from the Gentiles will be saved and attain blessedness. I have often had bitter experience of this incomprehension.

I do not think many Jews would object if the Messiah when he came again was the Jew Jesus. But wouldn't many Christians be uneasy if they found that the messianic ideas of the Old Testament prophets were fulfilled, even though the Old Testament is also Scripture for them?

And what about the return to Jesus himself? We know that Judaism has never rejected Jesus. The Council document also indirectly confirmed this. So for Jews a 'return to Jesus' can only be an answer to the question: was Jesus a good Jew? Anyone who reads the synoptic gospels without prejudice must answer Yes. And in fact especially here in Israel the preaching of Jesus is fruitful for Judaism itself. How much easier is the return to Jesus than for example Spinoza's problem, and he was certainly not a 'good' Jew.

III. JESUS THE JEW – A CHALLENGE FOR JEWS

We began with Lessing's distinction between the religion of Christ and the Christian religion. The distinction is too sharp but it has a typological truth. There are Christians who are chiefly concerned with living by Jesus' message in the gospels. There is another type of Christian who holds that 'he was more than a man' and make him 'an object of worship'. For the latter salvation through Christ is the important thing. But the number is increasing of the other sort of Christian who is drawn to the message of Jesus and is prepared to give up everything for the sake of this priceless treasure. In general a Jew only has access to Jesus through his words, not only because as a non-Christian the Christology usually seems foreign but also because the religion of Christ is a Jewish religion. The Jew recognizes a familiar tone of voice in Jesus. For a Jew the question is about the Jewishness of Jesus, a question both legitimate and genuine. Or, to put it another way, what Jesus himself thought about the Jewish religion is significant. Jesus is close to some Jewish religiously creative personalities and less close to others. The difference between the Christian who fulfils the religion of Jesus and the Jew, is in that the Christian is compelled to see the teaching of Jesus as infallible whereas the Jew can freely choose whether to accept the view of Jesus, as a Jew, or to criticize it. And even when the Jew is convinced of the rightness of Jesus' Jewishness he can still accept some of Jesus' teaching, perhaps adapt to and reject other parts of his teaching as not quite correct.

Thus Jesus is a question for a faithful and unprejudiced Jew. To Christians it may appear paradoxical that a Jew can learn from Jesus how he should pray, the true meaning of the Sabbath, how to fast, how to love one's neighbour and the meaning of the kingdom of heaven and the last judgment. An unprejudiced Jew will always be deeply impressed by Jesus' point of view. He understands he is a Jew speaking to Jews.

But there is something else to consider. St Augustine frequently said about the Jews and the Old Testament: 'They bear the divine signs for the salvation of the Gentiles, not their own salvation.' This is not very friendly. But let us accept it and extend it. The Jews bear not only the Old Testament but also, in a very limited sense of course, the New Testament, particularly the Jewish teaching of Jesus for the salvation of the nations. For the Jew, even if he is not very well-educated, can, because of his Jewishness, reveal aspects in the words of Jesus which Christians sometimes miss. And a Jew in the 'diaspora' can be of quite a lot of help to Christians. Jesus did not speak and work in empty space, and in order to understand him we should know what his circumstances were. Thus a Jewish background would make it easy for someone to understand that the Sermon on the Mount was not a utopian programme or a moral code for the elect. A Jew would never think that Jesus had put himself above the Law when he said 'I say to you that every one who is angry with his brother shall be liable to judgment' (Mt. 5.22). In the first place we can find Jewish parallels to this saying and in the second place the Jew knows that the saying does not weaken the prohibition 'Thou shalt not kill'. Is it certain that this is as clear to all Christians as it is to a Jew? Is it true that we cannot call it Christian when someone sees a murder — or a murderous threat to a whole people — and is not moved to anger? We cannot fall into such a sinful error when we read Jesus' words in a Jewish way. By Jewish, I mean here knowing what God asks of us: 'To do justice, and to love kindness and to walk humbly with your God' (Mic. 6.8). Jesus himself called this the main burden of the Law (read Mt. 23.23 and Lk. 11.42 together).

We should understand these words of Jesus in a Jewish way. If we do this it makes many things easier. If the Church were to teach like this its moral force would be so great that no one could resist it. I have tried to show how far Jesus can be a question for the Jews. In my opinion an authentic Jewish answer to the question of Jesus would also be important for Christians. Jesus refers the Jew to his Jewishness and the Jewish reaction to Jesus can perhaps help a Christian in his Christian awareness. How wise the Council was to say: 'Sacra haec Synodus mutuam utriusque cognitionem et aestimationem quae praesertim studiis biblicis et theologicis atque paternis colloquiis obtinetur, favere vult and commendare.' The Holy Synod wishes to promote mutual knowledge and respect which is the fruit above all of biblical and theological studies and fraternal dialogue.

Translated by Dinah Livingstone

2 What Meaning has the Fact that Jesus was Jewish for a Christian?

Bernard Dupuy

I. THE PERSON OF JESUS CHRIST

WHEN formulating this question it is important to insist that we are not interested only in finding out the consequences for Christian belief of the fact that Jesus was born a Jew. That basic affirmation, with all its implications,[1] is too restrictive as far as our present purpose is concerned. Nor are we limiting ourselves to the fact, well-established and acknowledged more than in the past, that Jesus received the usual Jewish *education*, in accordance with the rules prescribed by the Law.[2] While emphasizing the first signs of Jesus' vocation, the Gospel bears witness, when he talks to the Doctors in the Temple, to the fact that he belongs to the religious tradition of his people (Lk. 2.41-50).

But our discussion is not intended to refer solely to the origin, way of life or thought-patterns of Jesus, but to the concern of his public ministry when an adult, and to an event that was decisive for faith, as well as to the meaning that he himself saw it as having — his passion and resurrection.

Was Jesus Jewish in his whole being, in his entire behaviour and right up to the end of his earthly existence? Or did he at a certain point distance himself from Jewish life? Did he speak and act 'in conformity with the Torah', or must we see behind every sentence and word of Jesus, a claim that puts in question the very tradition of Judaism? Would it be in accordance with the faith of Chalcedon not only to state abstractly that he was man and God, but to say that he was a *Jewish man* and God?

I believe that the Gospel forces us to that point, and to accept all its implications we must remember that over the centuries many people, while not daring to deny it, have pretended to forget it. 'A lot of Christians knew that Jesus was a Jew, but think in some way that Judaism didn't play any part in his life, because he was a "Christian".'[3]

Because of this permanent dichotomy, there has been a tendency to separate the 'Jesus of history' from the 'Christ of faith'. This separation, which looms large in ecumenical dogmatic theology, has had a tragic effect on the faith of Chalcedon. Nowadays we are beginning to appreciate the reason for the gulf. The responsibility should not be laid at the door of historians or religious experts. Its origins should be sought for in the history of Christian dogma. Because the Jewish Jesus was forgotten, and to the great detriment of faith, theology allowed the entry of a 'Christ of Christian faith'.

Why is it so risky, considering the importance of the matter — to write a life of Jesus? We must remember from the start that it is a modern difficulty. The Fathers knew that it was enough to open the Gospels. They claimed that the Old Testament supplied the keys for reading them. But nowadays it is difficult for us — even on opening the Gospels — soberly, passively and without contention, to conceive of this *Jewish Jesus*, for our understanding of Jesus' Jewish environment is still very much marked by the controversies between Jews and Christians.

This 'return to the origins' is all the more sensitive when these controversies are grounded in the New Testament itself.[4] The Jewish *Sitz im Leben* of the Gospel often escapes is. One could quote numberless examples. For us the precepts of the Law are weak and ineffectual, whereas for Jesus and his contemporaries they were a source of life.[5] For us the pharisees are the epitome of 'pharisaism' but no longer of a spirit of loyalty and attachment to the Law widespread throughout the people.[6] For us the parables are edifying tales, almost timeless in character, whereas in fact they are full of expectation of the Kingdom.[7] In order to rediscover Jesus today, we have to understand the meaning he found in rituals, what signification he allowed the Torah, how he spoke about God to the crowds who followed him and to his disciples. We have to get back to the One who became incarnate as a Jew among the Jews; to the One for whom being a Jew was not some kind of throw-away garment but his very being.

To lay claim to faith in Jesus Christ while ignoring this essential fact would be tantamount to Docetism. The first tension in Christianity was that between Ebionism and Docetism. Ebionism disappeared without leaving any trace.[8] But in avoiding Ebionism the Christian faith hardly escaped Docetism entirely. It would be profoundly wrong to imagine that the realism and universalism of Christology have to do with the generality of the dogmatic formula. On the contrary, they have to do with its precise implication: its very particularity: it was in becoming incarnate in the Jewish people that Jesus offered himself as saviour to the entire human race. We can acknowledge Jesus only as he appeared to us: as *this* particular Jew, *this* just and suffering servant; it is *thus* that he reveals himself in order to reign over the world.

What we say about the person of Jesus should also be said of his message. If the kerygma of the Church is to have its full meaning, we have to refer to the Gospel as Jesus preached it. But that Gospel was preached in the language of the Bible, on the basis of the Torah, with reference to the Prophets, from the bosom of a tradition which was certainly discussed and analyzed but not rejected (Mt. 23.2-3). It was addressed primarily to the Jews, and even to the Jews alone: 'to the lost sheep of the House of Israel' (Mt. 15.24). If we ignore the Jewish context of Jesus' preaching, surely we empty the Gospel of its very content.

It is of course possible to object that if the Gospel of Jesus was essentially addressed to the Jews, the kerygma, founded on the Passion and the Resurrection of Christ, speaks of Jesus in different terms; it directs us continually beyond the 'Jewish' Jesus in order to show us that, from the start, and from before the creation of the world, 'God was in Christ' and through him brought about the reconcilation of all men. The central statement of the kerygma, according to which Jesus died 'for our sins according to the Scriptures', in spite of the scriptural reference, goes beyond the strict content of the Jewish faith. It proceeds from the decisive event which established the Christian faith. It is the interpretation of a unique historical event, which not only occurred in the context of Jewish history and in a general way concerned the Jewish people, but was accomplished by Jesus once and for all.

That is an understandable objection. But surely Jesus carried out this decisive act *as a Jew*? That is suggested by the legal inscription Pilate put on the cross, and proved by the quotations from the psalms spoken by Jesus during his Passion.

Often the following alternative query is put forward: Is the redemptive interpretation of the death of Jesus on the cross the mysterious climax of the Jewish faith, or does it constitute a new doctrine and, ultimately, one heterogeneous to Judaism? That is a false dilemma. If Christian theology were founded on a basis other than Judaism, how could Jesus have spoken himself of his imminent death and how could it have had any meaning for his disciples? Thus some Christian exegetes (and by no means the least) have sometimes misinterpreted the Jewish context of the Passion and the Resurrection, and denied that Jesus announced his death and himself foresaw his redemptive end.[9]

That is the conclusion to which we are forced. Faith cannot but acknowledge the 'Jesus of history'.[10] The keygma does not direct us to one who lies beyond the Jewish Jesus, as if Christ existed in a world inaccessible to our eyes, from which his Jewish nature had been effaced.[11]

II. THE CHURCH OF JESUS CHRIST

There is a second question: that of the Church. Jesus was a Jew. But not all those who believed in him were Jews. Quite early on there were non-Jews among those confessing the name of Jesus. They were not asked to become Jews because Jesus had been one. It is not a question here of returning to this basic problem as posed to the Council of Jerusalem and resolved on the basis of rules imposed by Judaism for the conversion of proselytes. The question necessitates an examination of what the Church is in essence as grounded on the 'reconcilation of Jews and Gentiles'. To do that I would have to see how the kerygma could be professed in common by men of different religious and cultural traditions. That would lead us to pose the question of the establishment of feasts, of liturgy, of the calendar — in short, the whole problem of the connexions between Judaeo-Christianity and pagan-Christianity in the primitive Church. I cannot enter into that debate here.

If he in whom we believe was a Jew, it is no accident as far as the economy of the Church founded by Jesus is concerned that the Church consists of 'Jews and Gentiles'. It is necessary that there should always be some men who witness to the 'Jewish approach' of Jesus and who reveal to the others, those of non-Jewish origin who have a non-Jewish approach to Jesus, what that Jewish understanding of Jesus might have meant and what it still might mean today. That was the particular purpose of Judaeo-Christianity. But historically it could not persist, and once it disappeared, that Jewish witness to Jesus could be given only by Jews brought up in the tradition of the people of Jesus. That witness cannot come only from Jews who confess Jesus Christ but from the entire Jewish people, who — by their own vocation — witness to the living and unique God among men. In order to recover today in full that Jewish approach of Jesus, in order to meet in his very existence the 'Jesus of history', we have actually to presume the existence of that intermediary.

The Church is not connected to the Jewish people by an initial graft and by the mere fact that it was from the Jewish people that it received the Book which enables it to confess Jesus Christ. It is not only linked to the Jewish people which is always actually in a position to listen to the voice of God to which that Book bears witness. It is linked to it because the Jewish people is the ever-present trace of the revelation which it presents to the world as a memorial (*zikkaron*).

To give consistency and meaning to all that I have suggested here, it would be necessary to develop positively what Augustine said: that there is a permanent witness to God offered by the Jewish people,[12] and that that is our providential way to the 'Jesus of history'.

Of course some readers will expect some more concrete lines of research to be offered here. It is easier to indicate a method rather than to list results. The actual image of Jesus will become more definite for us when we are familiar again with the Targumim, and when we have stopped imagining a hiatus between the Hebrew people of the origins and the 'Jewish people' of the second Temple period. Perhaps the twentieth century will be the one in which the Church recovers the Jewish world contemporary with Jesus which the discoveries of the Dead Sea area now bring closer to us.[13] A better appreciation of the biblical bases of the New Testament can certainly offer considerable progress in understanding of the Gospel. In some cases it could help to rectify errors of interpretation.[14] For instance, P. E. Lapide showed that in the Greek text of the New Testament there were a certain number of false readings or interpretations which could be corrected by just looking up the Hebrew.[15]

Even from that point we should be able to reach an improved understanding of God and man, and the religious universe of Jesus and his disciples. With the renewal of scriptural studies, the expectation of the kingdom which is at the heart of the preaching of John the Baptist and the Gospel of Jesus, had already been accorded a central place since about the beginning of the century.

But there is still a lot to be done in order to understand the profound meaning for the disciples of Jesus' messianic titles, and in particular the title of 'unique son' of God. That was not understood as an affirmation of direct kinship with God.[16]

The Bible should remain our inexhaustible source to be explored for a correct understanding of the mystery of Jesus. It would be wrong to believe that the Epistle to the Hebrews supplies the full interpretation of Scripture current in the first apostolic generation. That generation formed slowly, and even now we are far from having garnered the entire teaching of the *Testimonia*.

But if these researches remained the concern of the specialists, they would certainly come up against the problems which troubled the exegetes of the last century. We must never forget the profound Jewish tradition which brings us a living interpretation of the Bible, and which is the best guarantee of its understanding.

To acknowledge Jesus today is not merely to repeat the witness of those who confessed him before us. It is not only to rediscover, by always going back to the origins, the confession of faith of the early Church — whether Jewish or Hellenistic. To acknowledge Jesus is to accept, today as yesterday, that historic meeting 'of Jews and Gentiles' reunited and reconciled in him. The confession of Christian faith is constituted by the close conjunction of those two bodies of witness. The fact that one is in the minority and almost invisible, and that the other is in the majority and takes up the entire front of the stage cannot change the basic structure.

In answer to the constant appeal of the nations the Church should constantly return to its sources and try to understand Jesus on the basis of the Jewish tradition by which it is itself fed and from which it offered its Gospel to the world. The sole guarantee of the mission of the Church to the nations of the world is this perpetual return to the sources.

Translated by John Maxwell

Notes

1   Of course, at the beginning of this century, as Jules Isaac puts it, there 'was a curious collection of Germanic robots ready to prove that Jesus was not a Jew' (*Jésus et Israel*, Paris, 1948, p. 37). That shows the extent to which prejudice can affect exegesis even when it pretends to a rigorously scientific approach. The nadir of this school was reached by Houston Stewart Chamberlain in his *Grundlagen des 19. Jahrhunderts* (1899). He was followed by P. Haupt with *The Aryan Ancestry of Jesus* and a series of authors listed by J. Klausner (*Jésus de Nazareth*, Paris, 1933, pp. 130-34). In France H. Monnier was about the only one who allowed himself to go so far: 'Jesus was not, properly speaking, a Jew. He was a Galilean. That is not the same thing' (*La Mission Historique de Jésus*, Paris, 1906, p. xxvii). It is also worth recalling J. Hempel, in 'Der synoptische Jesus und das AT', in *Zeitschrift für AT Wissenschaft*, 1938, p. 9 (note the date): 'The respect of the Jews for the Torah is an immoral attitude in the deepest and most tragic sense of the word' (cited by H. J. Schoeps in *Revue d'Histoire et de Philosophie Religieuse*, 1933, p. 17, note 36). Without indulging in such excessive judgments, other authors are inclined to play down the Jewishness of Jesus on the pretext that he was born in Galilee. The Galilean Jews however were authentic·Jews. It was from Galilee that the various national sallies of the Jewish people were made.
2   There is a matter of interest in R. Aron, *Les années obscures de Jésus*, (Paris, 1960), even though it is not a work of first-hand scholarship. For a precise reconstruction of the historical background, the new English edition (in progress) of E. Schürer's *The History of the Jewish People in the Age of Jesus* (Edinburgh, 1973, one volume so far) is of value.
3   St E. Rosenberg, *Judaisme* (Ottawa, 1967), p. 12.
4   See the debates on this theme published by W. Eckert, N. Levinson and M. Stöhr, *Antijudaismus im Neuen Testament?* (Munich, 1967).
5   On Jesus' relation to the Law, see D. Flusser, *Jesus* (London and New York, 1969); B. H. Branscomb, *Jesus and the Law of Moses* (New York, 1930); W. Kümmel, 'Jesus und der jüdische Traditionsgedanke' in *Zeitschrift für NT Wissenschaft* (1934).
6   Cf. ultimately, J. Bowker, *Jesus and the Pharisees* (Cambridge, 1973).
7   Cf. J. Jeremias, *The Parables of Jesus* (London, new ed., 1963), even though Jeremias does not, I think, sufficiently emphasize the context of Jesus' final coming in the parables.
8   On the significance of Ebionism, see the works of H. J. Schoeps, *Das Juden-Christentum* (Berne, 1964) and *Aus frühchristlicher Zeit* (Tübingen, 1950).
9   Cf. H. Riesenfeld, 'Bermerkungen zur Frage des Selbstbewusstseins Jesu' in *Der historische Jesus und der kerygmatische Christus* (Berlin, 1961), pp. 331-3.
10   Cf. F. Mussner, 'Der historische Jesus' in *Der historische Jesus und der Christus unseres Glaubens* (Vienna, 1962), pp. 103-28.

11   Cf. S. Légasse, 'Jésus, juif ou non' in *Nouvelle Revue théologique* 86 (1964), pp. 673-705.

12   'Testes veritatis nostrae et iniquitatis suae' (Augustine, *Enarr. in Ps.* No. 22).

13   The material supplied by Strack-Billerbeck should be used with care. While waiting for a new summary account of this kind, a useful source is the *Compendium Rerum Iudaicarum ad Novem Testamentum*, ed. M. de Jonge and S. Safrai (Assen, 1974), *et seq.* See also the remarks of D. Flusser in 'Die konsequente Philologie und die Worte Jesu' in *Almanach für das Jahr des Herrn 1963* (Hamburg, 1963), and my preface to D. Flusser, *Jésus* (Paris, 1970); D. Daube, *The New Testament and Rabbinic Judaism* (London, 1956) (new edition, 1974).

14   See the attempt to reconstruct the figure of Jesus in G. Vermes, *Jesus the Jew* (London, 1973).

15   P. E. Lapide, 'Hidden Hebrew in the Gospels' in *Immanuel*, 8, No. 2 (Spring, 1973), pp. 28-34.

16   I. Levi, 'Le sacrifice d'Isaac et la more de Jésus' in *Revue des études juives* (1912), p. 156; D. Lerch, *Isaaks Opferung christlich gedeutet* (Tübungen, 1950). H. Riesenfeld, *Jésus transfiguré* (Copenhagen, 1947), pp. 89-96; H. J. Schoeps, 'Paulus und die Aqadath Jischaq' in *Aus frühchristlicher Zeit* (Tübingen, 1950), pp. 229-38; A. Jaubert, 'Symboles et figures christologiques dans le judaïsme' in *Exégèse biblique et judaïsme*, special issue of the *Revue des Sciences religieuses* 47 (1973), pp. 373-90.

VI The Future of Christian-Jewish Dialogue

1 A Jewish View

Uriel Tal

I. TOWARDS A THEOLOGY OF THISWORLDLINESS

ONE of the essential developments in contemporary Catholic theology is the Church's renewed confrontation with the realm of earthliness. The Church, so it seems to a Jewish observer, is more and more preoccupied with man's activity, with man's possibilities of shaping physical reality in relation to metaphysical criteria.

This trend in contemporary theology has been clearly pointed out in the second Vatican Council's *Pastoral Constitution on the Church in the Modern World* entitled *Gaudium et Spes*, in chapter 3 which deals with the theological significance of earthly affairs and their relative autonomy. Article 36 says: 'For earthly matters and the concerns of faith derive from the same God. Indeed whoever labours to penetrate the secrets of reality with a humble mind, is, even unawares, being led by the hand of God who holds all things in existence, and gives them their identity.'[1]

Similarly, the second chapter of that constitution, the chapter that deals with the theological dimension of the 'proper development of culture' affirms that 'when by work of his hands or with the aid of technology, man develops the earth so that it can bear fruit and become a dwelling worthy of the whole human family, and when he consciously takes part in the life of social groups, he carries out the design of God'.[2]

This concern with the realm of earthly things may pave a way toward a new understanding of Judaism, perhaps much more than the declaration of the second Vatican Council that 'what happened in his

80

passion cannot be blamed upon all the Jews then living, without distinction, nor upon the Jews of today'.[3] While *deicidii rea*, the question of the Jewish guilt of deicide, is entirely an internal question, one that ontologically or theologically is virtually impossible in Judaism, the renewed concern of the Church with the realm of earthliness has a common denominator with Judaism, with the *Torah* both as 'Law and Grace' and 'Law as Grace',[4] with The *Halacha* and consequently with the entire Jewish way of life. Thus, one of the essential concepts of Jewish religion is the term *Avodah* — literally in modern Hebrew 'labour', 'work' — which historically and theologically refers to 'sacrifice', and by extension to 'worship', 'service', 'prayer' and 'sanctification'.

II. HISTORICAL ROOTS AND COGNITIVE FORMS

This renewed and reaffirmed involvement of Christian theology with the realm of earthly things has its immediate historical roots in the teachings of a number of modern theologians, philosophers and leaders of social movements — such as Lamennais in the first half of the nineteenth century, Rosmini and Gioberti, Döllinger and Wilhelm von Ketteler and Adolf Kolping from the middle of that century on, and Loisy towards the end of the nineteenth and beginning of the twentieth centuries. As Thomas O'Dea has pointed out, these men attempted to work for the reconciliation of the Church and modern civilization.[5] A growing endeavour to come to terms with the modern world has been evident from the end of the nineteenth century on, when Leo XIII made his statements of social issues. This effort has continued until, as art. 23 of the *Constitution on the Church Today* declares, '. . . recent documents of the Church's teaching authority' which 'have dealt . . . with Christian doctrine about human society',[6] documents such as John XXIII's encyclical letter *Mater et Magistra* (May 1961), and *Pacem in Terris* (April 1963) and Paul VI's encyclical letter *Ecclesiam Suam* (August 1964). This development in theology culminates in those constitutions promulgated by the second Vatican Council which deal with the Church's relationship to the world, such as *The Dogmatic Constitution on the Church (Lumen Gentium)* and the documents that are addressed 'not only to the sons of the Church . . . but to the whole of humanity',[7] such as the *Pastoral Constitution* to which I have already referred and *The Declaration on Religious Freedom (Dignitatis Humanae)*. These documents, precisely because they refer equally to all human beings, religions, societies and nations — are of special relevance for the contemporary Jew, much more than those sections in which the old Christian-Jewish tensions are preserved. Perhaps this shift of emphasis may pave new ways toward reciprocal acquaintance.

The cognitive structure of this renewed preoccupation of theology with the realm of earthliness is a systematical continuation of the classic structure of the Church as a mystical unity. Accordingly, as St Ignatius Martyr in his *To the Magnesians* (13.2) would have it, the Church is at once an integrally *Societas fidei et Spiritus Santi in cordibus*, and *Societas externarum rerum at retuum*, a unity at once corporeal and spiritual. The relevance of concrete empirical and social realities and, according to arts. 73-90 of the *Pastoral Constitution*, even of political realities is gaining new recognition, and the responsibility of man for thisworldliness has been reaffirmed. At the same time, however, the Church has been explicit in emphasizing the limitations of earthliness. Thanks to its ontological status as the creation of God rather than man, earthliness, materialism or statehood should never have been exalted into the absolute.

This balanced approach, the affirmation of the world and the warning, according to art. 37 of the *Pastoral Constitution*: 'Be not confronted to this world (*Rom.* 12.2)', elevated the social concern of contemporary Christian thought into a struggle with one of the most delicate ontological difficulties inherent in monotheism. It is the dilemma between finitude and infinitude, empiricism and symbolism, thisworldliness and otherworldliness, also between the limitation and relativity of man's sovereignty and the moral responsibility of man's autonomy.

Quite a few theologians and Churchmen, especially since the times of Leo XIII's June 28 1881 *Diuturnum illud* on the origin of the power of the state and his November 1 1885 *Immortale Dei* on Christianity and the state, and of course his May 15 1891 *Rerum Novarum* on the condition of the working classes, have raised doubts as to the legitimacy, the wisdom or the theological consistency of this growing preoccupation with social, economic and political affairs. The discussions provoked by one of the central concepts in John XXIII's *Mater et Magistra*, the term 'socialization,'[8] may exemplify this inner conflict in contemporary theological circles.

Now it is no secret that the ambivalent feelings about thisworldliness and the doubts raised about the increasing tendency to acknowledge the evolutionary character of man and of history are frequently motivated by political interests, by power considerations, or merely by a widespread fear of change, both in doctrine and society. Yet it would be a grave mistake to narrow our view of this dilemma to those obvious political considerations. The deeper aspect of the dilemma is ontological.[9] It is a difficulty inherent in any metaphysical structure of thought and cognition which deals with limited, relative physical phenomena. The solution to this cognitive duality, to the tension between the earthly and the heavenly cities, between the natural and the spiritual order, in terms of incarnation and transformation, is of course unique to Christianity. But the need for a visible manifestation of the invisible God in the world and the concomitant danger of an absolutization of the world once God's revelation has been manifested, are shared by all true monotheists.[10]

Indeed, a careful analysis of the Documents of the second Vatican Council will show that those constitutions and declarations in which the human dimension has been emphasized are consistently counterbalanced. Thus, art. 25 of the *Pastoral Constitution* proclaims that 'man develops all his gifts and is able to rise to his destiny',[11] by faith of course, but also through 'social institutions, social life', through civic and political communities including historical nations and political states, culture, science, art and additional areas of human creativity. This statement is carefully complemented by art. 57 of the same constitution, in which the Church warns that 'man confiding too much in modern discoveries', may 'even think that he is sufficient unto himself and no longer seek any higher realities'.[12] While 'society . . . is of vital concern to the Kingdom of God',[13] man should worship God, the absolute, rather than himself, his own relativity.

III. RELIGION AND HUMAN CREATIVITY

Human creativity including socio-economic and political activity as arts. 63-90 clearly specify, is therefore recognized and even sanctified, not on its autonomous, human terms, and not in order to strengthen man's bondage to earth, to himself, to society, but in order to liberate man from his bondage, from his immediate, undifferentiated attachment to materialism. Freeing himself, by his own responsible activity and creativity, man will come closer to God, hence will develop '. . . himself as well'.[14]

On the basis of this underlying conception, human creativity has been affirmed in two spheres, the personal and the social. In the personal sphere, by unfolding his 'spiritual and bodily qualities' man 'goes outside of himself and beyond himself'.[15] Culture or science may free man both from his natural uncultivated surroundings and — as we learn from the *Declaration on Religious Freedom* and from the late John Courtney Murray's impressive commentary on it — from his enslavement to his own irrationality.[16] Human and social creativity have thus the potential of a man's exodus from his personal Egypt, from his estrangement from the Kingdom of God.[17]

In the social sphere man's work implies a continuing effort to bring the natural world under his control. This reaffirmed acknowledgement of the religious legitimacy of society and of the civic community has brought about a new emphasis on what art. 53 calls the 'sociological and ethnological' justification of the realm of man's creativity. More-over, the theological relevance of civic communities is applied, not to one culture but to a 'plurality of cultures', and to custom handed down not by one tradition, but by various ethnic traditions, so that ultimate-ly 'each human community' will be able to create 'its proper patri-mony',[18] freely and equally.

If, as declared in art. 53, the acknowledgment of this ethnic and cultural pluralism refers to all 'the men of every nation' and if a Jew too is acknowledged by the Church as man and as a citizen in his own nation, then indeed this renewed affirmation of the theological rele-vance of the world of creation, of life and survival, of existence and being, may render the traditional preoccupation of the *Torah* and of Judaism with the realm of earthliness more understandable, though not necessarily more acceptable to Christians.

IV. JEWISH FORMS OF EARTHLINESS

Judaism as a normative as well as a contemplative religion, as a people and as theology, Judaism in its legalistic and rationalistic as well as mystic and pietistic forms, is concerned less with the immanent mystery of God than with the ways in which God's immanence has entered history. Judaism is mainly preoccupied with the ways whereby God unfolds his indwelling presence in a dynamic and developing world, in our 'camps, in the midst whereof I dwell',[19] on the one hand and, on the other, with the daily commandments, with the commit-ments required by God's very immanence in the world, i.e., by God's self-exile into reality.[20]

According to the Jewish view – a view contrary to Christianity – this act of revelation did not occur in a karygma, nor through the establishment of God's kingdom in Christ and the proclamation of the Word made flesh, nor through his Spirit as manifest in the Church. In-stead, the theological framework within which that same human reality now reaffirmed by the Church is of primary concern for Judaism, is the *Torah*, in its comprehensive sense. Accordingly, the *Torah* includes the hermeneutical development of both the *Halacha*, involving religious, ethical, civil and criminal law, and the *Aggadah*, which includes the complementary moral teachings, theological speculation, legends, folk-lore, liturgical or mystical forms of articulation. A Jew is called upon to accept the yoke of this entire tradition with love as indicated by the order of the paragraphs of the 'Hear, O Israel' prayer, one of the most essential parts of the Jewish daily prayer book. The first paragraph (Deut. 6.4-9) is the acceptance of the yoke of the heavenly kingdom out of love of the Lord 'with all your heart, with all your soul, and with all your might'. Only then, after one reaches the love of God 'with all thy heart' i.e. with both soul and body, spirit and material, the good and evil inclinations, one is ready to accept the discipline of the legal part of the *Torah*, as indicated in the second paragraph of that prayer '. . . if you will obey my commandments' (Deut. 11.13-21).

Man, who is the highest result of Creation, the pride of the Creator, was appointed God's vice-regent on earth by the words spoken to the first man and woman: '. . . Be fruitful and multiply, and replenish the earth, and subdue it, and have dominion over the fish of the sea, and over the fowl of the air, and over every living thing that creepeth upon the earth' (Genesis 1.28). It is man's destiny to rule over the created world, not to withdraw from it nor to keep others from it; it is man's vocation to have dominion over reality, that is to bestow form and order and impose norms on the worldly spheres, including society, hence inevitably also on civic communities, nations and states.

The *Torah*, therefore, and consequently the entire Jewish tradition do not confine themselves to what is called 'theology' or to spiritualized values. Judaism, through the knowledge of God, prescribes man's relationship to creation, to things, to the land, not only to heaven. Hence the *Talmud* deals with the complete conduct of the life of man in all its mutlifarious relations and phases, with all the forms of everyday life, of the individual's conduct in his home and with his family; with forms of growth into manhood or womanhood and ultimately of aging and dying; with forms of human relations, economic activity and social justice; with forms of prayer, study and creativity; with forms of expression and articulation in matters of both faith and of action.

V. TOWARD THE FUTURE

The future of the Christian-Jewish colloquy then, depends on the readiness of the Christian to understand his Jewish partner on his own terms. This would mean first and foremost to understand that the Jew, if he remains faithful to his tradition, does not conceive theology as something separated or even different from the realm of earthliness, from man and community.

To the extent that such a separation is unavoidable in the eyes of our Christian partners, it should be realized that in the realm of pure theology the fundamental principle of Christianity, that Jesus is the Christ, the Messiah in whom 'in the despensation of the fullness of times . . . all things . . . both which are in heaven and which are on earth . . .' (Eph. 1.10) will have been re-established and reconciled (cf. 2 Cor. 5.18), is unacceptable to Judaism. Judaism cannot accept Jesus as the Christ in whom the Kingdom of God is revealed. Or, more precisely, as long as Judaism remains faithful to the tradition of the ontological all-inclusiveness of the *Torah*, it cannot accept the Acts of the Apostles proclaiming to '. . . all the house of Israel . . . that God hath made that same Jesus, whom Ye have crucified, both Lord and Christ' (Acts 2.36; cf. Hebrew 5.5 and Psalms 2.7). What makes the acceptance of this principle impossible for the Jew is not primarily the accusation of deicide, as the Fathers of the *Declaration to Non-Christian Religions* probably assumed, but the declaration of Jesus the man as Lord and Messiah.

This refusal to acknowledge the messiahship of Jesus cannot be explained by simply reiterating the ancient claims of 'Jewish stiff-neckedness'. The explanation is inherent in the structural-cognitive form of *Torah* hermeneutics. Judaism cannot accept an incarnated mediation between God and Man, between Creator and Creation, because according to the *Torah* God and his manifestations cannot be mediated, only interpreted. Not a Messiah but the *Torah* with its all-embracing earthliness, with its roots in timelessness and its revelation in history interprets the unity of God and Being, of the infinite Absolute and its finite creatures. Therefore while God is beyond any description, location or limitation, his creative power resides in the finite universe. While God is hidden, his mighty actions are transparent, not through a mediator but, according to Rabbi Ishmael, whose hermeneutics prevailed throughout Jewish history, in the *Torah* because it '. . . speaks in the language of men', and thereby maintains the unmediated presence of God amidst his Creation, on earth rather than in heaven.

It is at this point, at the point of our mutual concern for man's effort to bring the world itself under his control rather than in the realm of irreconcilable theological differences, that the Christian-Jewish dialogue, and hopefully also the Christian-Islamic-Jewish one, has its future.

Notes

[1]   *The Documents of Vatican II, with Notes and Comments by Catholic, Protestant, and Orthodox Authorities*, ed. Walter M. Abbott (New York, 1966) (henceforth: *Documents*), p. 234.
[2]   *Documents*, p. 262.
[3]   *Documents*, p. 666.
[4]   R. J. Zwi Werblowsky, 'Tora als Gnade', in *Kairos* (n.F.) Vol. XV (1973), p. 157.
[5]   Thomas F. O'Dea, *The Catholic Crisis*, Chapter III: 'Earlier Catholic Attempts at Modernization' (second edition, Boston, 1969), pp. 38ff.
[6]   *Documents*, p. 223; cf. Werner Osypyka, *Arbeit und Eigentum: X. Reihe, Christentum und Gesellschaft*, Vol. 3 (Aschaffenburg, 1965).
[7]   *Documents*, p. 200.
[8]   *Documents*, p. 224, note 74. Cf. p. 286.
[9]   Cf. George Schwaiger, ed., *Hundert Jahre nach dem Ersten Vatikanum* (Regensburg, 1970).

10   Cf. Nathan Rotenstreich, *Tradition and Reality – The Impact of History on Modern Jewish Thought* (New York, 1972), pp. 111ff. – On the relevance of this dilemma in contemporary Jewish-Israeli thought, cf. Uriel Tal, 'Jewish Self-Understanding and the Land and the State of Israel', in *Union Seminary Quarterly Review* (New York, Vol. XXVI, No. 4, Summer 1971), pp. 351-67. – *Id.*, 'Zur neuen Einstellung der Kirche zum Judentum' in *Freiburger Rundbrief*, Vol. XXIV (1972), No. 89/92, pp. 150-60.

11   *Documents*, p. 224.

12   *Documents*, p. 263; cf. p. 217, note 45.

13   *Documents*, p. 237.

14   *Documents*, p. 233; cf. Wilhelm Keilbach, 'Der Fortschrittsglaube des Marxismus' in *Der Fortschrittsglaube Sinnund Gefahren*, ed., Ulrich Schöndorfer, *Studien der Wiener Katholischen Akademie*, Vol. 3 (Graz, 1965), pp. 35-52.

15   *Ibid.*

16   *Documents*, pp. 672ff.

17   *Documents*, p. 237.

18   *Documents*, p. 259.

19   *Numbers*, 5.3; cf. *Exodus* 25.8,9.

20   Jacob Neusner, 'Talmudic Thinking and Us' in *Invitation to the Talmud* (New York, 1973), pp. 233-46.

2 A Christian View

Kurt Hruby

I. A FUNDAMENTAL CHANGE OF ATTITUDES IS NEEDED

I am not advocating excessive pessimism, nor do I want to deny the value of the genuine moves towards contact between Jews and Christians — they have already received due emphasis — but it is nevertheless undeniable that so far there has been no sign, or at least not much, of a real contact with Judaism. The essential condition for fruitful contact which could then lead to a further phase of understanding is *full and unreserved recognition of the other party's legitimate theological and existential autonomy*. In the case of Jewish-Christian relations, the full weight of a centuries-old theological attitude is an obstacle to such a recognition of Judaism by the Christian Church. It is true that our age, perhaps more than any previous one, is a period of rapid development and fundamental transformations in all areas of life, including Christianity. Nevertheless, we must be clearly aware that developments in external phenomena are not always a criterion of their acceptance on the level of attitudes. For this reason, it would be wrong to expect a deep-rooted anti-Jewish attitude which has become a tradition in the course of centuries to change completely in a few years.

In the first stage of movement towards such a change — which is not yet over — it has been and still is necessary to bring about a 'thaw' in relations between the Christian community and Judaism. (We should really say the Christian communities, since the problem affects them all in the same way.) There can be no doubt that this thaw received a powerful stimulus from the events of the second world war, though this stimulus is now showing equally severe signs of wear and over wide areas the thaw has been succeeded by a new frost. In addition, since the war many tragedies have occurred to divert interest from the fate of the Jewish people in the years 1939-45. However, the conscience of Christianity could not simply ignore these events and was forced — even if the process was rarely explicit — to face the question of its responsibility in them.

The impulse behind the Christian reaction was, in other words, primarily humanitarian, with no explicitly theological basis; it was not possible for Christian consciences to live with themselves without adopting an attitude to the tragedy of the Jewish people which had taken place in an area considered as 'Christian'. That was the main impulse behind the 'Declaration on Israel' of the second Vatican Council. That Christian consciousness itself was largely unprepared for it was clearly shown by the massive attacks to which this declaration was constantly subjected in spite of the vagueness of its theological content and its far from revolutionary character. As is well known, these attacks nearly destroyed it, especially when Pope John XXIII, for whom it had been a genuine human and Christian concern, died while it was in progress. A comprehensive survey would include a list of similar efforts within other Christian communities, which would show a situation largely comparable with that in the Catholic Church.

If these initiatives were to bring about a real meeting with Judaism after centuries of total rejection, they would have had to be supported on a firm theological base. For the most part this did not happen. There were many reasons for this. It must be remembered that many contemporary theologians received their formation at a time when the treatise *Adversus Judaeos* seemed to belong to the core of their Christian theology. The theory of rejection and substitution provided a convenient explanation of the Jewish phenomenon and made further thought unnecessary. And in the case of the younger generation of theologians it must be realized that as a result of the influence of this 'tradition' most theological faculties of many Christian denominations largely ignore the Jewish phenomenon as an active spiritual force, with the result that there is a fundamental lack of sensitivity to it. Nor should we forget how many difficult problems increasingly press in on theology today. In this mass the Jewish problem is seen at most as one problem among others, a side issue, precisely because, as a result of the whole historical development, there is so little awareness that it is basically a problem which has a permanent and direct bearing on the existence of the Christian Church. It is also a fact that the political situation created by the founding of a Jewish state in Palestine in 1948, the resulting conflict in the Middle East and the problem of the Arab refugees have prevented any deeper theological consideration. Political passions and *partis pris* have obscured the main issue and made reflection next to impossible.

II. TOWARDS A REAPPRAISAL

In fact any real meeting with Judaism is impossible without a clarification of theological premises on the Christian side. This is a difficult and delicate matter, but one thing at least is clear — the question is the significance for the Christian Church of *Judaism today*, not the Judaism of the past, whose significance no one, presumably, would dispute. In practice this means the questioning of the whole of the 'traditional' theology of Israel or, better, an admission and recognition that so far in the Christian communities there has been no such theology, that the traditional theses themselves have been much more the product of historical conditions than an expression of real theological data. If the whole significance of Judaism for the Christian community is really contained in Augustine's remark that the Jews are *testes iniquitatis suae et veritatis nostrae* (*In Ps. 58 Enarr.* 1, 21-22; *PL* 36-37, 765), then it is totally unnecessary to argue for a theological reappraisal and look for a meeting with Judaism. If this is the position, we must simply accept once and for all — as it was for centuries accepted — that, to adapt Aquinas, *antiquum testamentum novo cedat ritui*. That is to say, the 'old' Jewish order has given way to a new Christian one. Christianity has succeeded totally to the spiritual position of Judaism and so made it theologically superfluous. Of course we can still be 'modern' (a joke after Auschwitz, since the benighted Middle Ages never ventured on such enormities) and make the point that this theological situation does not entitle Christians to interfere with the lives or property of Jews, but nevertheless the dividing wall erected by tradition between Judaism and Christianity remains as solid as ever. The result is that Christian contacts with Judaism and individual Jews are purely humanitarian, with no particular theological basis.

What we must ask ourselves is whether the 'traditional teaching' will stand up to a critical and biblical examination, or whether it is in need of reform and must give way to a totally new view of the relation between Christianity and Judaism. It is no solution to put forward 'revolutionary' ideas which themselves turn out to be as exegetically and theologically indefensible as the formulations which go back to the patristic tradition. A solution will only come from totally serious theological work, which must be put in hand without further delay. If it is not, Jewish-Christian relations will remain in a state of more or less peaceful coexistance, but with the ever-present danger that external circumstances — such as the political situation in the Middle East at the moment — will seriously disrupt them and lead to a new 'freeze'.

Most serious theologians today feel that the 'classical' description of the relationship between Judaism and Christianity has become untenable and indefensible. But when it comes to withdrawing from them and working for a new approach, they all too often do nothing and become seized by a 'prudence' for which the weight of history must be largely responsible. It is hard to escape the impression — recently confirmed publicly by the reactions to the French bishops' declaration — that people fear that the whole structure of Christian doctrine will be made unsafe if attempts are made to do justice to Judaism and recognize it as a theological factor and a valid form of spirituality in the present.

III. PAUL'S STATEMENTS

The recognition I have mentioned, which is, as must be emphasized yet again, the essential precondition for a meeting with Judaism, requires a total abandonment of the traditional position, but this abandonment seems not merely possible, but even required, in the light of a number of biblical statements.

I am thinking in particular here of the statements in Romans 9-11. So clear and pregnant are they that it is quite impossible to dismiss them as a tactical move by the Apostle Paul to counter anti-Jewish tendencies in the Christian community in Rome. If they were, Paul would hardly speak of a *mysterium* (Rom. 11.25), that is, in the biblical sense of the term, a particular divine mystery about which revelation enlightens us. If we follow the accounts in the Gospels, and also other stray pieces of reasoning in Paul, we are left basically with a simple picture. According to this, the message of salvation in Jesus Christ was addressed, as a result of the whole process of divine guidance, to the Jewish people, and their rejection of that message is in one respect the 'fulfilment' of history and of the function of Israel, and at the same time a profound tragedy.

There can be no question of an attempt to deny this tragedy of salvation history. Paul himself, in Rom. 9.1-3 and the whole of Rom. 10, is the first to emphasize it. However, the full significance and scope of this 'tragedy' can only be understood *when it is considered and interpreted in the context of the mystery which the apostle reveals to us*. In this context, an attitude which we first described negatively as a 'tragedy' now takes on a firm positive aspect: even the negative attitude of the whole people of Israel towards the Christian message is a necessary aspect of the process of salvation as a whole. In reality Israel neither stumbled nor fell (11.11); its attitude was a necessity to bring the salvation which is in Jesus Christ to the Gentiles. From the point of view of the preaching of the gospel, the Jews, by rejecting the message inevitably appear as 'enemies' (11.28), but this hostility is necessary 'for your sake' (11.28).

Lest anyone should conclude from this situation that it is merely the initial situation of Christian preaching, Paul lays the greatest possible emphasis on the fact that this state of 'aloofness' on Israel's part will last throughout the whole of Christian history, 'until the full number of the Gentiles come in' (11.25). In this sense, then, Israel performs a permanent function in relation to the community of Jesus Christ, and what appears in one respect as Israel's 'trespass' in this respect turns out to be 'riches for the world . . . and riches for the Gentiles' (11.12), even the 'reconcilation of the world' (11.15). This means that Israel is not rejected or condemned. They are in full possession of all God's gifts (9.4,5) 'for the gifts and the call of God are irrevocable' (11.29). When Israel in this way has performed its function for the world and for the community of Jesus Christ 'all Israel will be saved' (11.26), and Paul compares this final stage to 'life from the dead' (11.15).

A consideration of the situation in the light of Paul's statements not only leads to a complete abandonment of the traditional theories of rejection and substitution, but also makes it possible and necessary to give *a positive interpretation* of the present existence of the Jewish people. To be able to fulfil their function for the Christian community, the Jewish people must preserve their identity and autonomy. What is this function? It can take many forms in relation to a Christian community which has largely lost its Jewish, i.e. its truly biblical, roots, and for which the rediscovery of these roots in Judaism could be an important part of its reawakening and recovery in a period in which all 'systems', including theological ones, are being questioned. That is to say that actual Jewish existence can be seen as a necessity for Christianity, and on this basis a genuine encounter with Judaism can take place, an encounter based not merely on humanitarian but also on profoundly religious motives.

IV. FROM CONTACT TO COMMUNICATION

If this contact is to grow, slowly and organically, into communication, it is of supreme importance for the Christian side to learn to accept the Jewish people with all its aspects and manifestations as a datum and respect it as such. Christians must learn to understand Judaism as it is, and to stop trying to dictate the form of its existence by criteria laid down as postulates of Christian theology. This was the approach of the so-called 'Beirut theses'. This implies making the effort to see things as Judaism sees them as a result of its particular experiences, with particular reference to the national and spiritual renaissance which began with the founding of the State of Israel. This, of course, does not mean adopting some political position or approving any particular attitude of Israeli policy where it seems to conflict with biblical principles of law and justice. But Christians must learn that it is their duty, both because of the shared origins of Judaism and Christianity and because of the continued role allotted to the Jewish people in God's plan, to follow all that happens in and to that people with a keen interest, without feeling called to sit in judgment on the way of life of the Jewish people in our own day. As the Bible says: 'But Israel is saved by the LORD with everlasting salvation; you shall not be put to shame or confounded to all eternity.'

From a theological and religious point of view, the meeting with Judaism in the first phase and coming to terms with it in the second are implications of Christianity itself. That is a fundamental point. The theological work done under this inspiration must aim at clarity about what is involved by the actual correlation between Judaism and the Christian community in the whole period of the *tempus Ecclesiae*, and therefore now. It must try to elucidate Paul's words: 'it is not you that support the root, but the root that supports you' (Rom. 11.18). Only a full recognition of the necessary and lasting complementarity between Judaism and Christianity 'until the full number of the Gentiles come in' can produce among Christians a real change of attitude in their basic approach to Judaism and so lead to a true meeting and understanding.

Translated by Francis McDonagh

CONTRIBUTORS

LOUIS JACOBS is Rabbi of New London Synagogue, London, England, Lecturer in Talmud at the Leo Baeck College, and the author of several books and articles.

WILLIAM DAVID DAVIES has taught in English and American Universities and is at present G.W.I. at Duke University, USA. He is author of a number of published works.

JOSEPH HEINEMANN is Senior Lecturer in Rabbinic Literature at the Hebrew University, Jerusalem, and the author of books and articles in Hebrew and English.

CLEMENS THOMAS is Professor of Biblical Science and Judaic Studies in the Faculty of Theology of Lucerne University, Switzerland.

SAMUEL SANDMEL is Professor of Bible and Hellenistic Literature at the University of Cincinnati, Ohio, USA, and General Editor of the forthcoming annotated version of the New English Bible.

JAN MILIČ LOCHMAN is former Professor of Systematic Theology and Philosophy in the University of Prague. He is now Professor of Systematic Theology in the University of Basle, Switzerland, and the author of several works on Christianity, Marxism and secularism.

JAKOB J. PETUCHOWSKI is Research Professor of Jewish Liturgy and Theology at the Hebrew Union College and the Jewish Institute of Religion in Cincinnati, Ohio, USA, and the author of several books on prayer, liturgy and theology.

JÜRGEN MOLTMANN is Professor of Systematic Theology at the University of Tübingen and the author of several works on theology.

DAVID FLUSSER is Professor at the Hebrew University in Jerusalem in the Department of History of Religions. He is the author of many works on Judaism, the Dead Sea Scrolls, and Jesus and the New Testament.

BERNARD-DOMINIQUE DUPUY is Director of the Istina Study Centre in Paris and the author of several works on fundamental theology.

URIEL TAL is Professor of Jewish History at Tel-Aviv University, Israel, and the author of several works on Christianity, Judaism and anti-Semitism.

KURT HRUBY is Director of the Judaism section of the Paris Ecumenical Institute and Professor of Rabbinic Hebrew and Judaism at the Catholic University of Paris. He is Editor of *Judaica*.